THE WIFE OF
WILLESDEN

THE WIFE OF WILLESDEN

Incorporating:

The Wife of Willesden's Tale

which tale is preceded by

The General Lock-In

and

The Wife of Willesden's Prologue

and followed by

A Retraction

Told in verse couplets
Translated from the Chaucerian into North Weezian

Zadie Smith

PENGUIN BOOKS

PENGUIN BOOKS
An imprint of Penguin Random House LLC
penguinrandomhouse.com

First published in Great Britain by Hamish Hamilton,
an imprint of Penguin Random House UK, 2021
Published in Penguin Books 2023

The Wife of Willesden was first presented by Kiln Theatre in association
with Brent 2020, London Borough of Culture, on the occasion of the
Brent 2020 pilgrimage and celebration.

LIBRARY OF CONGRESS CATALOGING-IN-PUBLICATION DATA
Names: Smith, Zadie. Wife of Willesden. |
Chaucer, Geoffrey, –1400. Wife of Bath's tale.
Title: The wife of Willesden : incorporating: The wife of Willesden's tale,
which tale is preceded by The general lock-in and The wife of Willesden's
prologue and followed by A retraction, told in verse couplets ; translated
from the Chaucerian into North Weezian / Zadie Smith.
Description: New York : Penguin Books, 2023. | The Wife of Willesden was
first presented by Kiln Theatre in association with Brent 2020, London Borough
of Culture, on the occasion of the Brent 2020 pilgrimage and celebration.
Identifiers: LCCN 2022053805 (print) | LCCN 2022053806 (ebook) |
ISBN 9780593653739 (paperback) | ISBN 9780593653746 (ebook) |
Subjects: LCGFT: Theatrical adaptations. | Verse drama. | Poetry.
Classification: LCC PR1872 .W54 2023 (print) | LCC PR1872 (ebook) |
DDC 822/.914—dc23/eng/20221122
LC record available at https://lccn.loc.gov/2022053805
LC ebook record available at https://lccn.loc.gov/2022053806

Printed in the United States of America
1st Printing

Book design by Lucia Bernard

Dedicated to the *Windrush* generation,
with much love and respect

Contents

Introduction
From Chaucerian to North Weezian
(via Twitter)

This is a weird one: sometime in early 2018, I got an email from one Lois Stonock, informing me that 'we' had won the bid to be London's Borough of Culture 2020. I'm ashamed to admit it took me a minute to work out who this 'we' was and how I was included in it. Then I remembered: a year earlier I'd agreed to add my name to Brent's bid although to be honest I had only the vaguest sense at the time of what I had said yes to, or what I would do if, out of the thirty-two boroughs of London, my beloved Brent somehow beat the statistical odds and won.

Brent won. Lois's emails picked up in their frequency. Would I write something about The Ends to celebrate The Ends? But this simple request proved difficult to manage. It was like being asked to breathe when breathing is sort of what you do on the regular. Everything I write is more or less about Brent, yet being explicitly *asked* to write about Brent sent me into a spiral of self-consciousness from which no writing seemed likely to emerge. Poor Lois kept emailing. The deadline crept closer. I worked myself up into a panic. Brent, I'd say to myself, as I sat at my desk, *Brent*. Brent! Brent? I tried getting more specific: Kilburn. The Kilburn High Road. So long, so wide and so old. During the writing of a novel of mine, *NW*, I'd read a lot about the Kilburn High Road and its history, and knew it was Celtic originally, then Roman, then Anglo-Saxon, with an ancient river buried deep beneath it. Once a part of Watling Street, it was a common route for medieval pilgrims, on their way to visit the shrine of St Albans, or the Black Madonna in St Mary's, Willesden. Some of those pilgrims no doubt took their rest at Kilburn Priory (est. 1134), a famed local nunnery of Augustinian canonesses. Yes, the especially pious pilgrims would have stopped there. But surely many more people – basic types like you and me – would have paused in one of the pubs, like the Red Lion (1444) or the Cock Tavern (1486) for some ale and a pie and a bit of chat . . .

One day, just as I received another anxious email from Lois, it happened that I spotted a copy of *The Canterbury Tales* on a shelf in front of me and, at a loss for what else to tell her, I spontaneously suggested that perhaps I could take this connection between Kilburn and Canterbury pilgrimages and translate the original Chaucer into the contemporary local vernacular: *The Brondesbury Tales*. Cute idea. But when I actually took down the Chaucer I was reminded that his tales are many and long and it might take me till 2030 to complete the task. Well, how about *The*

Wife of Bath? Alas, this, too, was long. Well, how about a few verses of it, like a short monologue, the text of which we could put in our excellent *Brent Magazine,* or maybe even have a local actress perform it at the Kiln Theatre? Such was the plan.*

About a month later, I was heading to Australia for a literary festival when Lois emailed me about approving a press release. But the attachment was taking too long to open on the bad airport Wi-Fi, so I said I was sure whatever it said was fine and I got on that plane. A day later I landed in Australia and opened my laptop to find dozens of emails – from friends, family, colleagues and some strangers – all eager to hear more about my 'first play'. Not having written a play – or ever considered writing one – I was understandably a bit perturbed. I phoned my agent, who also congratulated me on my first play, and suggested I take a look at Twitter, which was apparently full of still more people almost as surprised as I was to find I had written a play. I then tried blaming Lois, but indeed in her press release she had said nothing about a play, although perhaps the word 'monologue' was, in retrospect, easily misinterpreted. I sat for a while in Sydney Airport and looked deep

---

*Of course, nothing about 2020 went to plan. Brent 2020 – like so many other cultural events of that year – was radically transformed by Covid-19, and the play itself cancelled and delayed.

into the gaping void in myself where a play was meant to be. I went through my options: break own leg, contract short but serious illness, remain in Australia, explain to Twitter it was mistaken, or try to translate a fourteenth-century medieval text written in rhyming couplets into a contemporary piece about Kilburn . . .

Which is all to say, when I sat down to write *The Wife of Willesden* I had no idea it would end up being one of the more delightful writing experiences of my life. I think, when we talk about 'creativity', not enough is said about the interesting role that limits, rules and restrictions can play. In this case, the rules of the game were almost absurdly constricting: a medieval text – concerning sexual politics that would seem as distant as the moon – constructed in rhyming couplets from lines of ten syllables each. Yet from the moment Alyson opens her mouth –

> *Experience, though noon auctoritee*
> *Were in this world, were right ynogh to me*
> *To speke of wo that is in marriage*

– I knew that she was speaking to me, and that she was a Kilburn girl at heart. What started out as homework soon came to feel like a wonderful case of serendipity. For Alyson's voice – brash, honest, cheeky, salacious, outrageous, unapologetic – is one I've heard and loved all my life: in the flats, at school, in the playgrounds of my childhood and then the pubs of my maturity, at bus stops, in shops, and of course up and down the Kilburn High Road, any day of the week. The words may be different but the spirit is the same. I loved the task of finding new words to fit. But just because you're enjoying writing something doesn't mean – in my experience – that it's going well. Here Indhu Rubasingham, the formidable artistic director of the Kiln, was vital, both as first reader, dramaturgical advisor and final judge, for it would be up to Indhu to decide whether this play that she had neither asked for nor expected was a) actually a play and b) suitable for her theatre. So that became my new day job: turning Alyson from Bath into Alvita from Willesden, while trying to maintain Chaucer's beautiful colloquial flow, those ten-syllable lines that rhyme without heaviness, and sing without ever actually becoming music. Chaucer wrote of the people and for them, never doubting that even the most rarefied religious, political and philosophical ideas could be conveyed in the language the people themselves speak. I have tried to maintain that democratic principle here.

When the play was finished, and Indhu decided to stage it in full – and for more than the single night I'd imagined – I don't think I have ever been more astounded in my life, nor more thrilled. To me, the Kiln is a sacred space: as a child I took drama lessons there, back when it was still the Tricycle, and I remember mourning the disastrous fire, and sharing in the local delight when a new theatre rose out of the ashes. I had so many of my earliest seminal theatrical experiences here. The Kiln is where I saw *The Colour of Justice*, about the Stephen Lawrence inquiry. It's where I first saw *Playboy of the West Indies*. The only way I could make sense of adding myself to the history of this storied stage was by remembering that it's really Chaucer up there – I'm only hiding in the folds of his garment.

It must seem, to many, an odd partnership. When I started writing, it often felt that way to me, too. The distance between Canterbury and Kilburn, and between the fourteenth century and the twenty-first, looked epic. But I wasn't very long on the road before the sympathetic rhymes between the two became audible and then deafening. 'Sovereigntee' began to sound a lot like 'consent', for example, and Alyson's insistence on physical pleasure not unlike the sex-positivity movement, while her contempt for class privilege feels uncannily close to our debates on that topic today. Even the act of sexual violence that sits shockingly at the centre of her tale – and the restorative justice Alyson offers as a possible example of progressive punishment – read, to me, as absolutely contemporary. But that all makes it sound as if Alyson is a dogmatic sort, keen to impart serious moral and social lessons to her audience. Nothing could be further from the truth. Alyson shares with my own Alvita (I hope!) a startling indifference to the opinions of others and a passionate compulsion to live her own life as she pleases.

She has nothing to hide. Her desire to dominate men she freely admits; her own occasional hypocrisies she does not disguise; her insatiable appetite for life she announces to all. Personally, I could listen to her day and night, but having been to the theatre myself, and being aware that audiences generally prefer plays to involve more than one person, I made the decision early on to parcel out some of Alyson's scattershot wisdom and opinions to the various other people she speaks about, for and through.

Still, despite the fact that Alyson has turned into Alvita – and then been split many times over into all her husbands and friends – the text is, for the most part, a direct transposition of the Wife of Bath's prologue and tale. Here and there I have made judgement calls, substituting contemporary references for ones I thought too obscure to be meaningful to contemporary audiences. For example, the Pardoner, the Summoner and the Friar – all of whom make brief appearances in the Wife of Bath's prologue – have been transformed, respectively, into their modern vocational equivalents: a charity chugger, a bailiff and the minister of a local megachurch. I have also taken a few liberties with the structure. All of Chaucer's tales are framed and bookended by the opening General Prologue and the final Retraction; the same is true here, but I have radically paraphrased – and mercifully shortened – both. The greatest change, perhaps, is in the tale itself, which has been switched from Arthurian England to eighteenth-century Jamaica. Try as I might, I couldn't imagine Alvita using King Arthur as a point of reference. These transformations aside, I'm proud to call the Wife of Bath and the Wife of Willesden half-sisters. I've so enjoyed my time with both of these wild women. I'd like to claim Alvita is the more feisty of the two, but the truth is you'll find all her feistiness in the original. That said, she certainly is more Kilburn and more Jamaica. She nah easy and she talk her mind.

Dramatis Personae

In order of appearance

ALVITA, THE WIFE OF WILLESDEN *A Jamaican-born British woman in her mid-fifties*

AUTHOR *A brown woman in a headwrap*

PUBLICAN POLLY *The woman who runs the Colin Campbell pub*

AUNTIE P *Alvita's churchgoing aunt*

PASTOR JEGEDE *A Nigerian minister at a North London megachurch*

KELLY *Alvita's very shy niece*

HUSBAND NO. 1, IAN *An older, white Englishman*

HUSBAND NO. 2, DARREN *A young, good-looking bwoy*

HUSBAND NO. 3, WINSTON *A Rastaman*

HUSBAND NO. 4, ELRIDGE *A well-to-do gentleman in his fifties, of Caribbean heritage*

HUSBAND NO. 5, RYAN *A Scottish student doing his Masters*

GOD

ST PAUL

BLACK JESUS

ZAIRE *Alvita's best friend*

COLIN *A charity chugger in his early twenties*

SOPHIE *Colin's fiancée*

NELSON MANDELA

ASMA *Local rebel wife*

SOCRATES

ERIPHYLE *A bad wife of legend*

ARRIUS *A vengeful husband of legend*

BARTOSZ *A local bailiff*

STAGEHAND 1 *A child*

STAGEHAND 2 *A child*

QUEEN NANNY *Our Maroon hero of Old Jamaica*

YOUNG MAROON *A soldier in Queen Nanny's army*

OLD WIFE *An Obeah woman of advanced years*

The same actors play:

Author, Kelly, Zaire, Eriphyle and Queen Nanny

Publican Polly, God and Sophie

Auntie P and Old Wife

Pastor Jegede and Husband Elridge

Husband Ian, St Paul, Socrates, Arrius and Bartosz

Husband Darren, Colin and Young Maroon

Husband Winston, Black Jesus and Nelson Mandela

Incidental characters and choruses are
played by members of the cast.

THE GENERAL LOCK-IN

We are inside the Colin Campbell, a small pub on the Kilburn High Road. The sun is setting on the celebrations of the announcement: Brent is to be the Borough of Culture for 2020. People are pouring into the pub for refreshment and rest. A large banner above the bar reads: 'The Kilburn High Road Pub Crawl'. Another sign reads: 'BRENT BOROUGH OF CULTURE: 2020'.

The Campbell is a quiet pub, usually occupied by a few all-day lone drinkers, but today these old men in their wrinkled suits are suddenly inundated by a colourful crowd. There's been dancing; some people are in carnival-like costume; there are people in their national dress, families, teenagers, lovers. Every possible kind of person. The bar staff struggle to serve the influx of people and seat them all, but after a bit of kerfuffle, most have a table, and now begin opening packets of crisps, or their own tubs of home-made food . . .

There is, in one corner, a little makeshift stage, with a home-made sign hanging behind: 'Celebrating Local Stories'. A red-headed young man with his back to the audience has

*a video camera on a stand, ready to film whoever comes up
to talk – but people seem reluctant. Music is playing, footie
is on the TV, we can't hear the people, but we see lots of
little local dramas and conversations playing out, and may
notice one especially striking woman,* ALVITA, WIFE OF
WILLESDEN. *She's settling seating arguments, she's hand-
ing over pints to people who can't reach the bar, laughing and
joking with everyone . . .*

In one corner, the AUTHOR *sits, quieter than the rest,
with a laptop on her table.*

AUTHOR
It was the summer of 2019.
I was back home, checking the local scene
And the whole neighbourhood was in the streets
To celebrate the recent local feat:
Winning the London Borough of Culture.
Call it a pilgrimage: all together
We crawled down Kilburn High Road, until we
Reached the Colin Campbell. We drank. Polly
Bailey, who runs it, suggested a

WHOLE CAST
LOCK-IN!

PUBLICAN POLLY
Let's get our drink on with the whole block.
And, wait, listen: here's what we're gonna do:
From right now till . . . let's say . . . half past two
We'll have a little contest. Your stories
On that stage. I'll be the judge and MC.
And when everyone's told their tale, the best
One will receive a full English Breakfast
Tomorrow morning, on the house. *With* chips.

All cheer.

AUTHOR
Everyone got on their open-mic tip . . .
We had all types of people in that night,
Young and old, rich and poor, black, brown and white –
But local: students, merchants, a bailiff,
People from church, temple, mosque, shul. And if
There's a person in Brent who doesn't think
Their own life story isn't just the thing
To turn into a four-hundred-page book
I'd like to meet them. So off they went. Look
At them.

*We see people encouraging each other up to tell short stories
from their life, and the reaction of the crowds.*

All telling their stories. Mostly
Men. Not because they had better stories
But because they had no doubt that we should
Hear them. The night wore on. I wondered: Would
A woman speak? And one or two did. But
Like the men – like most of us – they said what
They thought others wanted to hear. Or lied,
Or humble-bragged, or said the nice, polite
Clichéd things that nice people like to say . . .

*We see a man and woman on the stage together and we hear
the following snippet.*

FEMALE SPEAKER
He's just 'the one' – we get married in May.
He's like my rock? Wouldn't you say so, Steven?

MALE SPEAKER
Yeah: everything happens for a reason
And we're just meant to be! Our stars aligned.

FEMALE SPEAKER
It's Fate! (Our gift registry's online.)

AUTHOR
Some said 'brave' things that took no bravery
To say, or were dull, or didn't move me –
Or spoke about their 'journeys' with an air
Of triumph. I was starting to despair . . .
Then I saw Alvita. That is: the Wife
Of Willesden. And the story of her life's
Worth hearing.

RYAN
Tho' she's a bit deaf herself
In one ear . . . but otherwise in good health.

WINSTON
And skilful! Makes her own clothes, every stitch.
That's not Armani – that's Alvita!

ASMA
                              Rich
She is not. But she never passed a *Big
Issue* vendor without chucking a quid
Their way.

WINSTON
Cuss you if *you* don't.

ZAIRE

                Fake gold chains
Are her jewellery of choice. She drips like rain.

DARREN
Her underwear is dramatic – and red.
Like the soles of her knock-off 'Choos'. It's said
She looks bold. She gives side-eye perfectly.

ZAIRE

       She's been *that bitch* since 1983.

RYAN
And yeah, she's been hitched five times to five men.

WINSTON
(Without counting back-in-the-day bredrin.)

ASMA
But we don't need to get into that now.
She's a well-travelled woman. She allows
Herself adventures. Self-care is her truth.
She's been Ibiza, Corfu, Magaluf.

DARREN
She likes to wander. Hates to be tied down.
With that gap-toothed smile she strides around town
Dressed to impress.

ZAIRE
     Wears an *isicholo*:
A big Zulu hat. She's not Zulu, no . . .
But let woman have her hat!

WINSTON
                  And a skirt
That shows her shape.

DARREN
And them shoes that will hurt
You if you're in her way.

ASMA
        She's not just fierce
Though. She's sweet and wise. Cupid's dart has pierced
Her so often, she's an expert on love.

DARREN
Been there, done that. This one knows it all, bruv.

We see ALVITA *being ushered towards the little stage, but she refuses it, and instead takes her rightful place, centre stage in the Colin Campbell. The pub turns black: there is a theatrical spotlight upon her. But before she speaks, the scene freezes while the* AUTHOR *gives her Chaucerian apologia . . .*

AUTHOR
But before she starts, a word to the wise:
Not a trigger warning, exactly, but
A proviso: it's not my tale. I just
Copied it down from the original.
I could make stuff up and rewrite it all
But that would surely defeat the purpose,
And if Alvita does make you nervous
It's worth remembering – though I'm sure you know –
When wives spoke thus six hundred years ago
You were all shocked *then*. The shock never ends
When women say things usually said by men . . .
And one last thing: if you spot yourself and
Think I've made you posher or more common
Than you'd like: sorry. I've got a good ear,
But I can only write down what I hear . . .

THE WIFE OF WILLESDEN'S PROLOGUE

ALVITA *reanimates and the* AUTHOR *withdraws to her table. Throughout the Prologue,* ALVITA *regularly breaks the fourth wall, speaking to the real audience as much as the pub one. Her accent is North Weezy with moments of deliberate poshness as well as frequent lapses into Jamaican patois and cockney for comic effect. She is a world-class raconteur. She begins:*

ALVITA
Let me tell you something: I do not need
Any permission or college degrees
To speak on how marriage is *stress*. I been
Married five damn times since I was nineteen!
From mi eye deh a mi knee.* But I survived,
Thank God, and I got to say, of the five,
None of them were total wastemen. But last
Week . . .

....

*Patois: 'From back when my eyes were at my knees.' That is, 'Since I was a small child.'

At this point the lights come up again, but there is something surreal about the new lighting in the pub, as if we are in a magical, liminal space between storytelling, memory and reality. The pub people react and laugh and groan like an audience, but they are often roped into the performance, too. Some of these moments are explicitly noted below, but a director should feel free to use the PUB CHORUS *to animate and dramatize as many of Alvita's stories as they see fit.*

I'm with my Auntie P, yeah, and she starts
In on her Bible talk:

AUNTIE P

                Yuh nuh know Christ
Him a wedding guest one time in him life?
In Cana, Galilee? Please, niece, beg yuh
Tell me what you do the opposite for?
How come you believe you can get wedded
Five times? Lawd knows how many times bedded!
Tink when Jesus met the Samaritan,
By dat well: 'member how he cuss her, man,
Him seh, 'Woman, you been married five times
Already.' You can't say *this man ah fi mi*
Because nutten nuh go so. Not at all.

ALVITA
And I was like, look, Auntie, you can bawl
Me out, but I still don't even get why
He said that? She married the first five guys.
So why not six? Is there a set limit?
With me, I'm almost fifty-five, innit,
And if there *is* a right number of men,
That's news to me. Is it six or eight? Ten?
In my view, people got too much to say;
They chat rubbish. But from my Bible days
I know it says:

We hear church music and see church lighting, and we meet
PASTOR JEGEDE *in the middle of a sermon.* AUNTIE P
and KELLY *are listening intently.*

PASTOR JEGEDE
            'Go forth and multiply.'

ALVITA
I remember the bits that weren't too dry . . .
And isn't it that God said when they married:

PASTOR JEGEDE
A husband must leave his old family,
And link up mind, body and soul—

ALVITA

With me! Yep. Nothing about bigamy
In there, or more-gamy-than-that (cough, cough).
So how come some people slagging me off?
Nah, I'm not having it. Count the pickney
And women of Marley. How 'bout Stevie?
Now, you know Stevie's had more than one wife!
Blindness don't stop him enjoying his life.
I should be so lucky as Bob Marley.
Rita? Miss Jamaica? He had plenty
Woman, and I'm sure he had a good time
With them all, back in the day. And that's fine.
But let's also thank God for *my* five men:
Ian, Darren, Winston, Elridge and Ryan.

As this is said we see Alvita's husbands, IAN, DARREN,
WINSTON, ELRIDGE *and* RYAN *– who are dotted around
the pub – stand up and start looking at each other curiously.
We may not notice that the fifth husband,* RYAN, *is the red-
head with the video camera, who we can't really see: the video
equipment obscures his face. When he stands it must look as if
he is just doing something to his camera. After a moment they
sit back down again.*

(You think five's a lot? I could've had ten!)
But I'm well choosy. I actually picked them
For their *ass*-ets, different for each person.
One went to the College of North West London,
Two went to the School of Hard Knocks. The sick
Thing about Kilburn is how we can mix
It up with anyone? High, low. Posh, poor.
We've had practice. We'll walk through any door.
And that's like me spending my time studying
Five different husbands. You learn many things . . .
And, honestly, I'm up for Number Six
Whenever, wherever he feels to pitch
Up. Serious: if Five drops dead, boom, like that:
I won't wait for my hymen to grow back.
That's not me. You'll soon see me on Insta
Chucking the bouquet to the next sista . . .
Pastor, if your man dies, you're free, innit?
To get hitched again, if you feel like it.

PASTOR JEGEDE *looks like he doesn't want to concede this point; also these questions are disturbing his service, which, in a parallel reality, is happening throughout.*

Auntie P, isn't St Paul the one who said

AUNTIE P
Better to be married than burn up dead!

ALVITA
But in your church, the one on Willesden Lane

We hear church music again, and see AUNTIE P *and her* SONS *praying in the pub, with* PASTOR JEGEDE *leading the prayers.*

The old Bingo place, you go fill your brain
With judgement. Pastor chatting all that breeze:

PASTOR JEGEDE
. . . Wicked Lamech, whose sin was bigamy . . .

ALVITA
How come Jacob and Abraham marry
Again? And I'm sure Pastor put a ring
On it a few times in Nigeria . . .

AUNTIE P
All I know is that the Lord God him nuh
Like looseness. Him defend de marriage bond.

ALVITA

Yeah, but Auntie, the thing is, that's just wrong?
Where do you think you read that? The Good Book?
You can't show it to me. S'not there. I've looked.

AUNTIE P

Me know him defended virginity.

ALVITA

Now hol' up, hol' up, my dear Auntie P:
Thing is: I can read just like you can read,
And I'm telling you no. It's true Paul said
He didn't want us having sex for fun –
But it weren't like: COMMANDMENT NUMBER ONE.
Auntie, what you call laws I call advice!
A guideline. And they all sound very nice,
But everyone got to make their own choice
In life. And if God in his big God voice
Was like:

GOD

Everyone. Asexual. NOW.

ALVITA

It wouldn't make no sense. Because then how's
He expecting to make more pure virgins

When there's nobody to give birth to them?
Please. At least St Paul wasn't all about
Cancelling things God himself hadn't called out!

PASTOR JEGEDE
We aim for chastity. This is the prize.
The contest is to be pure in God's eyes.

KELLY, *Alvita's very nerdy, shy and put-upon niece, dares
to raise her voice:*

KELLY
But that's not, like, meant for . . . well, like, maybe –

ALVITA
Yes, girl – g'wan – *say* it! (That's my niece, Kelly.)

KELLY
Maybe that's not meant for everybody?
Like, Mum, maybe God makes some people true
Saints, yeah? But with some he's like: s'up to you . . .
Like, I totally get Jesus was pure
And he was into that but are you sure
It's got to be like that for me and you?

ALVITA
This is what I'm saying! Kelly, *thank* you.
Bottom line, Auntie, I have permission
From bloody St Paul himself to go fishing
For husbands when and where I feel like it.
The only thing I'm willing to admit
Is you probably have to wait till one dies
Before you move on, because bigamy-wise
That'd be an issue.

PASTOR JEGEDE
               It is clearly
Said, by the apostle, that purity
Is best.

ALVITA
Yeah, but he was chatting about
Himself! St Paul be like:

ST PAUL/HUSBAND IAN
  I won't go out
With you. I will not come back to your place.
I won't submit to your sinful embrace.
We're not 'getting it on' on your sofa.

ALVITA

A holy man plus a supernova
Like me? You put us together? There will
Be fireworks, you get me? There just will.
But their church says:

AUNTIE P

                    Best to sleep with no one!

ALVITA

Wait – check it:

PASTOR JEGEDE

                    But if you marry someone –
And this is true for our women and our men –
It is best never to have sex with them.

ALVITA

Jokers. Fools. But it don't even touch me.
I don't mess with churchmen *or* my family.
My thing is: you want to think you're a saint?
Fine. But don't slut-shame me because I ain't
About that. It's not like I'm pretending
To be picture perfect. Or curating
My life for others. Despite what you see
Online, we're not all on yachts in Bali.

Some of us are on the ninety-eight bus
Which comes on time, and that's enough for us . . .
Auntie, I think God loves variety,
That's my belief. Cos if he *did* make me
He set my soul on its own strange path. Plus
Maybe he gives out sex like Santa Claus:
The nice get no sex drives; the nasty . . . more.
Maybe it just depends. Maybe if you're
Asexual or abstain he's into that . . .
That'd make sense cos his son was like that –
But you make everything so literal!
You really reckon Jesus meant to tell
Us all to be as broke as him? Nah. He's
Just saying:

BLACK JESUS
        You can be brassic like me
If you think you can handle it, but 'low
It for everybody else.

ALVITA
           For real, now,
Them rules are for the girl who feels that she's
Perfect. And that blatantly isn't me.
As you see, I'm in the prime of my life
And right now I'm into being a wife.

My kind of wife. Cos, tell me, Auntie P.
This equipment between our legs which we
Carry: why d'we have them in the first place?
Or you reckon it's some kind of mistake?

AUNTIE P
Wat a way yuh like fi argue me down!
But I believe our . . . private parts . . . they around
Fi two purpose. Fi pass the urine. And
Know who ah woman and who ah man.

ALVITA
Auntie's a comedian. But she knows
Well from experience how these things go.
It's crazy to me that Pastor gets mad
When I talk about women's pleasure and
The idea that if there *is* a God he
Can't hate on his own gift, which he must see
Is not just for making babies or . . . wee.
Pastor, it's right there in the book! Let's read
It:

PASTOR JEGEDE
'Man owes a debt to his wife.'

ALVITA
In bed!
That is literally what the man said!
And to pay that sexual debt in full,
You usually need your own genitals.
Look: my point is, we're given these things
For more than childbirth and urinating!

ZAIRE, *Alvita's best friend, raises her hand.*

ZAIRE
But just cos you have working genitals
We don't *have* to go down the kid road? All
Of us don't need babies. It's cool if your
Road is kids. But that's not all these are for.

ALVITA
(My bestie, Zaire.) And then there's Jesus:
So pure and holy he's just not that fussed
Re sex. And I've got nothing against pure,
Holier-than-thou people. I think you're
All great. But there's a lot of different kinds
Of women in this world. Some like red wine
Thirty quid a pop. You know who you are!
I'll take a shot of Baileys at the bar.
I'm that kind of girl. Not fancy but fun,

Like Baileys. Sweet. And I get the job done.
My thing is, to be honest, I'm just real.
I do and say exactly what I feel.
I'm not fussy, but I stick to my guns
And in *my* marriage I'll use *this* for fun.
If it's God's gift, I best use it that way!
Cos if I waste it, what's God gonna say?
Now, husbands: I was and am here for you:
Tonight, tomorrow. But you need to do
Something for me first. I demand pleasure.
That is your debt to me. It's not pressure,
Exactly, it's about consent. You'll agree
To owe me love, good sex, and that when we
Marry, your body and soul will be mine
As long as we're a thing. From that time
Till we're done, your body is my playground,
It's for me, not for you. I've just found
That really works for me? In fact, St Paul's
The one gave me the idea. Cos he's all
About

ST PAUL
'You husbands! Love your women well, day in
Day out!'

ALVITA
Thank you! That's all I've been saying!

*There is applause from the tables, but some consternation, too,
especially from some of the men.*

Any questions? Comments? So far, so clear?
Yes, you: don't be shy. Loud – so I can hear.

COLIN, *a nervous young man in a charity chugger outfit,
stands up. His fiancée,* SOPHIE, *sits beside him.*

COLIN
Hello . . . well, my name's Colin . . . I work for—

ALVITA
You hassle fools in the street for cash – sure –

COLIN
Well, actually I raise money to fight—

ALVITA
You get their sort codes. Make them feel all right
About themselves. Mug them for a good cause.
But tell me: how can I help you and yours?

COLIN
Um . . . well, this is Soph, we just got engaged . . .
And a lot of what you said tonight made
Me feel a bit anxious, if I'm honest.

ALVITA
Is it. Go on . . . I don't bite, I promise.

COLIN
Like, are you saying that if I marry
She owns me? I find that a bit scary –
Like, in my view, that's taking things a bit
Too far, like: sexism – but reversing it?

ALVITA
I see, Colin. Thing is, though, my story's
Not even started yet? So don't worry:
Try not to wag the tail before the dog.
This bit's just the – whadyacallit – *Prologue*.
I'm about to drop knowledge on you,
Colin, and on your lovely girlfriend, too.
Because I've been there, Colin; this ain't my
First rodeo. And I'm using my *time*,
My *precious* time, to help needy men
Like you, not to make total fools of them

Selves in marriage. That is my mission.
Best thing you can do? Sit up and listen.

COLIN
Yes, Ma'am – I mean, Miss – I mean, Mrs – Miz?
Of course, I know you know your business,
Wife of Willesden – I shouldn't interrupt.
You know what? I'll own my privilege – and shut up.

ALVITA
Young men: if you think you can stand to hear
Some truth I'll tell it. But if you start to fear
I'm running my mouth, talking wild and rough,
Or I've said too much, please don't take the huff –
Or get offended; don't be *that* guy . . .
I might take the piss – but I'll tell no lies.
So let's get down to it: those men I've had?
Three of them were good and two were bad.

We see the FIVE MEN *identified as she mentions them, but
again, that* RYAN *is one of them remains unclear.*

ALVITA
The three good ones were – bad news for Colin –
Older. They'd already found their place in

This world. But they had their work cut out
In the bedroom, because I'm all about
Pleasure, and they couldn't always keep
Up with my desire. They needed their sleep.
To be honest, it didn't bother me.
They made up for it in maturity.
With these young'uns you need a magic potion
To get their love, respect and devotion.
Back when I was young I worked way too hard
For approval; I'd put all my damn cards
On the table. Now I have no need. Since
I hold them in my hand. I can rinse
Out their bank accounts, move into their
Flats – they'd give me all, if I asked. But where
And when and why should I be asking
For love? The sun is out: I am basking
In affection. Meanwhile they have work
To do up in the bedroom. Learn to twerk,
For example: that's a useful skill in

Here we might see a number of older men in the PUB CHORUS
trying to master this task.

A man. That's something really worth learning!
But the older dogs are less
Inclined to learn; they want to get their rest.

Fine. But I still ruled them with a firm hand.
I cussed them daily, and they'd understand,
And be grateful, *so* relieved, when I turned
Nice. And that's one key thing I have learned
About marriage. You've got to treat them mean
To keep them loving and humble and keen.
Let me break it down: when a husband
Shows his cards; you've got to hide your hand.
Before he gets on your case, get on his.
I'd be like: first thing, handle your business.
What were you doing at that girl's place?
Are you really going to say to my face:

HUSBAND DARREN
I went to check my cousin — he's crashing there.
Didn't really notice . . . what's her name? Claire?

ALVITA
Bruv, I've seen her: fake nails, fake boobs, fake hair —
You're gonna do me like that? Is that fair?
And then meanwhile, if I'm just jamming
With a male friend, you're sure we're banging,
You lose your mind, cuss me up and down . . .
Double standard! But that's what I've found
About husbands. They chat too much breeze
About women. Got way too many theories.

I've heard them all.

HUSBAND WINSTON
                    Don't trust a gold digger;
They've got plans for you. Dem fine figures
Are a trap, yuh know? Dey ah go reel you in.
You'll pay in cash; it's the wages of sin.
Not love they want, man, it's alimony.

ALVITA
And then there's:

HUSBAND IAN
                    Avoid the ones with money:
They'll emasculate you. When a man
Earns less than his wife you'll find he can't
Respect himself. That's not just my view,
That's in evolutionary science, too.

ALVITA
Yeah, yeah, yeah. And if she's very pretty
God help her.

HUSBAND DARREN
                    Must be doing you dirty,
Because no one that fit could be faithful—

ALVITA

According to you. For some men it's awful
If a woman is rich or hot or fine
Or smart or talented or sweet or kind –
Cos that means someone else might want us.
And everything you once loved about us
Becomes the problem. If we still attract
Attention, then:

HUSBAND ELRIDGE

     You ask for it. The fact
Is, it's your fault.

ALVITA

     If we no longer do,
That's worse. We might go grind on a fool
'Pon the dance floor just for attention.

The pub becomes a nightclub and we see ALVITA *joyfully
dancing with a number of her* HUSBANDS *and others.*

And then slyly, casually, he mentions
That he can't remember why he chose
This. He could be playing Tinder. Who knows
How sweet life could be if he were free?
But deep down? It's all insecurity.

Some husbands are wound up way too tight.
Some of dem on that jealousy tip night
And day:

HUSBAND ELRIDGE
            The thing about women is they
Act a certain way up until the day
You wed. Then it's a whole other story.
New becomes old. Fresh becomes boring.
The pink cammy gets switched for grey cotton . . .
All that tear-your-clothes-off sex? Forgotten.

ALVITA
And so on. He'll say:

HUSBAND ELRIDGE
                        When a man buys clothes
He gets to try stuff on before he goes
And buys it. With wives? You roll the dice and see!

ALVITA
Honestly, sometimes this man made me
Want to scream. And he'd try to turn it round.
He'd say:

HUSBAND ELRIDGE

       The truth is you love the sound
Of men singing your praises. You call
Yourself a feminist but you want all
The compliments all the time. If you say
How does this look? am I free to lay
It on the line? Come on now. We both
Know my duties. I've got to swear on oath
You look like Angela Bassett. *All*
The time. For your birthday you want a ball.
You want me to hire out Camden Palais
And pay for it all. Then you want me to say
I love all your girlfriends, even that one
Claims she's a 'life coach' but lives with her mum.

There has been much laughter in the pub and music and re-enactment during ELRIDGE's *speech but now the lighting becomes stark and everything is silent as* ALVITA *offers her rebuttal.*

ALVITA

Husband Number Four, you *lied*. Tell these
Good people how sometimes nothing could please
You. When the green-eyed monster took over
You weren't yourself. You forgot we were lovers.
You'd rant and rave. You thought poor young Ryan

35

The student kid – the freckled Scottish one –
With his dark red hair and his tiny bum

RYAN, *who's the kid filming, raises a hand to the audience,*
to be acknowledged, but we get no sign that there is anything
between him and ALVITA.

You'd say I'm eyeing him like I want some
Of that? Please! Not if you died tomorrow!
Meanwhile, you won't even let me *borrow*
The keys to the Subaru! You act like
What is yours is not also mine. You psych
Yourself out, stressing about who owns me,
While you keep your junk under lock and key.
And try to keep me home. But we don't own
Each other. I don't check up on your phone,
Or use GPS to see where you are.
But seems you'd like me locked up in that car!
You *should* be saying:

ALVITA *gets behind* ELRIDGE *and uses him as a ventrilo-*
quist's dummy so her voice seems to come out of his mouth while
she controls his movements.

ALVITA (*AS ELRIDGE*)
>   Alvita, you do you.
Go out and find your joy. I won't do
Anything to block or kill your spirit
Cos I love you and I trust you, innit.

ALVITA
Women like me, we can't love control freaks.
We want to travel, to live, to seek
Fresh pastures, possibilities, new worlds.
We're women. Not children. Not little girls.
The best man of all, blessed and wise, is dead:
Nelson Mandela, cos it's him who said:

An old man in the PUB CHORUS, *one of the old regulars
we saw in the opening scene, turns from his pint and takes on
the role of* NELSON MANDELA.

NELSON MANDELA
Resentment is like drinking poison

ALVITA
>   Yuh see?

NELSON MANDELA
And then hoping it will kill your enemies.
And the wisest men know how to rise above
The desire to control the ones you love.

ALVITA
Husbands! Hear these words! Know them to be true.
If you get yours, why d'you care what I do?
Are you lacking something? Are you deprived?
Come sundown, aren't you truly satisfied?

We see ALVITA *sidle up to the* AUTHOR *with her mobile.*
She seems to be asking to jump on the Author's Wi-Fi hotspot,
but the AUTHOR *isn't having it.*

It's like them people who lock up their Wi-Fi . . .
Like, they think it's gonna run out! Like if I
Jump on it, and get something for free,
It's unfair. Not as far as I can see.
Just mind your own business, husbands! Then
I'll mind mine. And peace will reign in Willesden.
But they don't. He's in my face about what
I wear. He's like:

HUSBAND ELRIDGE
         Please God tell me you're not
Going out in that. The skirt's way too small;
The top's too low; you're barely dressed at all.

ALVITA
And I wait and dare him to speak some more.

HUSBAND ELRIDGE
I'm just saying sometimes you look like a—

ALVITA
STOP RIGHT THERE. Please don't use, my brother,
One type of woman to cuss another.
We are all sisters. And don't try to neg
Me. You feel free to take me down a peg
Or two. Mention my crow's feet. Cellulite.
Tell me I'm boring or not too bright.
Cos you've worked out when I'm shy or sad
I won't stray too far. I won't act too bad.
But when I'm feeling myself; hair done right,
Clothes on point? Then you nuh want me out nights.
When I hit the club, it's full of your spies:
Your cousin, your sister's man. Benny. Mike.
You think your *man dem* can shut *me* down?
Step to me; we'll see who ends 'pon the ground!

And he sees I'm not playing. Then he frets
And feels sorry for himself:

HUSBAND ELRIDGE
                                    Don't get
Married. Only two things worse than a wife—

ALVITA
Cue some lame-arse joke about pain and strife . . .
The same sad anti-wife jokes you see online –
What would you'all do without us for punchlines?
You get so dramatic:

HUSBAND WINSTON
                                    To love you is hell –
It's like I'm thirsty and you're a dry well.

ALVITA
So *you* say

HUSBAND DARREN
                        It's like being on actual fire –

HUSBAND IAN
Like being thrown on a funeral pyre

HUSBAND ELRIDGE
You're like woodworm

ALVITA
Says *you*

HUSBAND ELRIDGE
     And I'm the tree.
You're not done till you've eaten all of me!

ALVITA
People of Brent: you hear how he talks when
He's pissed? Well, I *told* him he said that then
I used it against him. He never found
Out it wasn't true – I just wrote it down
And said he did. That poor fool got no peace.
I told student Ryan, and Kelly, my niece,

We see KELLY, *and see* RYAN *still hidden by his camera
raise a hand, but again in the most casual way.*

And they believed me and blamed *him*; he looked
Like the bad guy and I'm off the hook.
Simple advice, Colin, it'll take you far:
Whoever's behind the wheel drives the car.

That's it. We didn't fight, if I'm honest.
He planted his seeds. I burned his forests.

HUSBAND ELRIDGE
I said sorry for things I hadn't done!
Girls I never touched, game I never run.

ALVITA
I knew you too ol' to be playing away
But I accused you of it anyway
Because you liked it! You needed jealousy
To feel I wanted you like you wanted me . . .
I told you: 'All my going out at night
Is just to check those girls I fear might
Be after you!'

HUSBAND ELRIDGE
        And I truly believed.

ALVITA
You were way too vain to think I'd deceived
You. But truth is I'm just out getting mine!
And the thing is, I get my way every time . . .
Women are good at lying! Or if you
Want to say it more nicely, we just do
A little creative work with the facts.

I cry, I make up stuff, I blatantly act –
I'm playing four-dimensional chess,
Colin, and no husband can ever mess
With me. Especially not in a bed.
That's where I truly eff with their heads . . .
For example, if I've got a new man –
A fresh husband; not a flash in the pan –
Lying next to me, and here comes his hand,
I immediately make him understand:
I will get out of this bed unless you
Get me off first. *Then* I'll see what I can do
For you. The point is you don't get someting
For nutting. No, my friend: that's not a thing.
And honestly, as it goes, I was not
Attracted to any of those old men. But
I put on a good show. And they gave me
What I was owed, and to speak honestly
I probably stressed them all the time
Because I really hated having to grind
Them at all. But you know what? Even if
The Pope was watching, I'd still call them chiefs,
And fools and eediat. And Christ himself knows:

BLACK JESUS
Even if she went and died tomorrow
No one could say she didn't do her share

Of work in the bedroom. And to be fair
To the husbands, I should mention, Colin,
They did try. To get it up, to put it in . . .
They'd roar like lions, crazy with lust
But every time they tried – it was a bust.

ALVITA *is grateful for* BLACK JESUS*'s intervention on
her behalf.*

ALVITA
Then I'd say:

We see the following acted out between ALVITA *and*
HUSBAND IAN. ALVITA *starts kind and loving, works
herself up into a comical rage, and then just as abruptly turns
philosophical:*

Oh, babe . . . little man looks small
Tonight. Come here. Kiss me. Don't be all
Down about it. You're always telling me
To take a chill pill. Relax. And just *be*.
So take your own advice. Calm yourself.
Be patient! How come you got all this wealth
But can't get it up? Don't get an attitude!
I'm just saying – I'm not trying to be rude.
Why're you groaning? You wanna get with me?

Mi deh yah* – I'm right here. Now, you see,
Fact is this pum-pum† could have a good
Time somewhere else – don't mean to kill the mood –
But apparently if I cheat on you
That would make me a 'bad wife' and 'a shrew'.
Lawd! The patriarchy! It's like I'm caught
In a trap and it's all your own damn fault!
Oh, we'd have a lot of these little chats . . .
Let's move on. Fourth Husband. We'll get into that:
My fourth husband was a proper player.
We were married but he had a lover.
And I was young, and really feeling myself.

HUSBAND ELRIDGE
Body tight, no one left *her* on the shelf –
Stubborn and wilful; first one on the dance
Floor and last one off.

ALVITA
                    If I had a chance
To sing I took it. Sweet soul voice I've got
When I'm pissed. When I've had a few shots.

---

*Patois: 'Everything is good, I'm here, I'm okay.'
†Patois: crude term for 'vagina'.

Me nah braffing.* No, man, I sing like a bird –
Not like these uptight churchy men I've heard
Threaten their wives with hell if they want drink!
If any man thinks he'll stop *me*, best think
Again! Because a Baileys with nuff ice
Gets me in the mood. Makes me feel nice.
And I'm not going to stand here and tell you
That I'm not more likely to want to do
It when I've had a few.

ALL THE WOMEN IN THE PUB
                            Let's all be real.
Sometimes a drink or two helps seal the deal.

ALVITA
Oh, Lawd Almighty! When I think back to
Them days when I was young, I can't do
Nothing but smile. I love to remember
That sweet May time, now I'm in September . . .
I'm still glad I had my time in the sun!
Now I'm old. Boobs hang low. Lost my bum.
But you know what? It's really whatever.

....

*Patois: to boast or take excessive pride in something.

PUBLICAN POLLY
Youth and beauty, they don't last forever.

ASMA
The sweet fruit's gone, there's no juice left behind.

ZAIRE
But I'll still squeeze whatever's left out of the rind!

ASMA
Or, at least, I'll do the best that I can.

ALVITA
But wait up: back to this fourth husband.
To be honest, I got my screwface on
When he chirpsed other women. But I won
In the long run. I didn't cheat but I
Got my flirt on, my come-to-bed eyes . . .

HUSBAND ELRIDGE
Couldn't stand to see her with another man!

ALVITA
Jealousy fried you in your own damn pan!
Oh, I made you a proper hell on earth . . .
This man who bitched like he was in childbirth

If he even stubbed a toe. Not good with pain
That one.

HUSBAND ELRIDGE
And God knows she made me insane
With agony.

ALVITA
               He died not long after
I got back from holiday in Jamaica.
He's buried near here, just by Uncle P
Up Willesden Lane, in that old cemetery.
The headstone's plain as a plate, not my taste –
But paying more for that one'd be a waste,
You get me? Anyway, he's now deceased.
So farewell and God bless him. Rest in peace.
My fifth husband. Okay, here we go. Well,
I actually *don't* hope he rots in hell.
And yet, to be honest, he was the worst.
He'd get physical with me. That's the first
And last time I'll let that happen, I swear.
He hurt me here, there, oh, everywhere . . .
And yet in bed he was so fresh, so fine,
Gave head with such skill, the man took his time,
So even when I was aching from old
Bruises, I could turn his base love to gold.

Can it be I loved him more than the rest
Because he always gave me so much less?
The thing with girls – I'm gonna generalize –
Cos I've noticed it, and I sympathize:

PUBLICAN POLLY
What we can't get easy? That's what we crave.
We get obsessed, we stalk, we don't behave . . .

ZAIRE
Tell us no, we're all over it, we're set:
But come on strong? We lose interest, all bets
Are off. Play hard to get, and we'll chase you,
But act too keen? Then I'm just not that into
You. Masochism, some say, but isn't it
Also just how things work in a market?
Love is capital: this, smart women know.

ALVITA
But I married the fifth one, as it goes,
For love not money – bless him – still a young
Bwoy he was; an Oxford student, just sprung
From college and looking for a flatshare.
He rented a room off my mate Zaire,
My ride-and-die bitch. I tell her everything,
And vice versa. There's no secret I can't bring

Zaire. If my husband pissed up a wall
Or something much worse, it's Zaire I'd call,
Or any girlfriend I know, or my niece,
Kelly . . . He can't make me sign a release
Form! I'll speak! And that's what I kept doing,
Telling his secrets, and he was screwing,
And well-shamed and sorry he ever told
Me any private thing, new or old . . .
But then one day mid-March, it was springtime –
Which is when I like to take some proper 'me time'
At Zaire's; get out of Brent; see some trees
(Cos sistas like the country, too, believe);
And we hung out with this Ryan, Zaire
And me,

ZAIRE
Running round Oxford, here and there;
'Spose we felt we could let our freak flags fly
Hang wid da yute; and, maybe check some guys . . .

ALVITA
But who knew what was in the stars for me?
Where, when and who would be my destiny?
I was just doing my thing: clubbing, nights
Out at student parties; or downing pints
In their weird country pubs, or out raving,

ZAIRE
And always in her tight red dress, leaving
Not a thing to the imagination.
No need to wash it – she always had it on . . .

ALVITA
But let me tell you how it went down:

ALVITA *approaches* RYAN *and starts flirting with him, as she tells her story. Romantic music plays, birdsong: 'Loving youuu . . . is easy cos you're byooootifuuuul . . .'*

Me and this kid, flirting; alone, far from town,
And one day I just say to him, look, man,
If my husband dies, we should make a plan
To marry, okay?

Sound of record being violently ripped off turntable. PUB CHORUS *are a bit scandalized to realize Elridge was right about Alvita and Ryan the whole time.* ALVITA *tries to defend herself, like someone on the* Jeremy Kyle Show.

                    Cos, people of Brent:
It's about insurance. And in the event
Of . . . *whatever*, I never get married
Without a little something up my sleeve:

Like a good plan B. You don't want to be
That dumb mouse who thinks it's gonna get free
Through the only hole it found in your home –
The same one you just filled with toxic foam . . .
So I told him I loved him like crazy!
My mother taught me that – a smart lady –
I said I dreamt of him regularly,
But in these dreams it seemed like he'd killed me

*This tragic, bloody fantasy is acted out, and then, just as
quickly, is revoked.*

Because the bed was totally bloody –
Blood on the sheets, all over my body –
But that's a good sign, cos in the Tarot
Blood's a symbol for gold, far as I know –
But it was all lies! Trust me, I don't waste
Time dreaming of men. That was cut and paste
Out of Mum's playbook. She's my true mentor
When it comes to husbands – and so much more.
But wait – Colin – I've gone and lost my thread –
What was I saying? Right – fourth husband: dead.
And when I saw him laid out at James Crook

The pub turns into a funeral parlour.

I got my weep on, and really did look
Gutted, like a proper sad widow should,
And wore a veil. But since I was all good
For husbands, with one lined up round the bend,
I didn't really cry that much, in the end.

ZAIRE
The church service was St Mary's, next day.
Full of local mourners from down our way,
And student Ryan was there in the crowd

ALVITA
And God help me, but I was like *wow*
He's fit, you know! Nice body, tight round bum . . .
He was twenty. I could have been his mum.
Yeah, I was forty, to tell you the truth,
But he's a honey, and I've a sweet tooth –
Plus I'm gap-toothed like Madonna; which suits
Us both; symbolizes passion; it's cute,
It's sexy, and Christ Almighty, I *liked* sex,
I was hot, young-ish, horny, full of next-
Level energy, and had – so husbands
Told me – the best punani in the land!
I'm one of these Venus-born girls for real,
But I've also got this Mars side? I feel
Like Venus gave me my lust and passion,

But Mars made me a woman of action.
Basically I'm Venus with Mars rising,
Which is why I don't get this 'slut-shaming'?
It's sad: I'm just doing me, naturally:
I follow my stars, and they have made me
Unable to ever say a hard no
To a nice, fit bloke who's good to go.
And plus, here's the mark of Mars on my face
(I've got another in a private place)
Which means even though Auntie prays for me,
It does no good. I can't choose carefully.
I'm all instinct. It's whatever feels right.
He can be tall or short or black or white –
I'm not bothered, as long as he feels me.
Don't have to be rich, or have a degree . . .
What can I say?

ZAIRE
                          Something like a month passed
And Al and Ryan got hitched. It was vast,

The pub turns into a wedding.

That wedding, they did it in proper style,
And then she signed over to him the pile

Of money, two flats, and the Subaru
That she'd got from leaving the previous two.

ALVITA
Truth be told, I lived to regret that choice.
Ryan, turns out, was a dick. Raised his voice
At me over every likkle ting, left
Me no freedom. See this ear? I'm now deaf
In it, cos he smacked me in my head
For tearing a page from a book he'd just read.

ZAIRE
But he couldn't keep her down. Al's a lion.
Stubborn. And not scared of chiefs called Ryan.
She still cussed him day and night and flexed where
She felt like flexing. Traipsing here and there,
Going round the old flats, which he *hated* –

ALVITA
And he'd start giving off to me, slated
Me, giving it all this 'bout his mate, Mo,
Who spotted his wife in the street with no
Veil on and left her like that!

We see RYAN *bringing* ASMA *to tell her story, like an example in an argument.* ALVITA *is unimpressed, as is* ASMA *for being thus used.*

ASMA

                    High and dry,
Haven't seen him since two thousand and five.
Good riddance!

HUSBAND RYAN

                    But what about Ibrahim's
Wife? Went Olympics without asking him.

ASMA

Two thousand twelve. He left. And she's okay!

ALVITA

He'd even dig up the Bible. He'd say:

HUSBAND RYAN

Actually, in Ecclesiastes, there's
Some really quite sensible stuff. Like where
It says: 'Thou shall not let thy wife wander
About.'

ALVITA

　　　　I saw he was getting fonder
Of his own voice. Liked to make pronouncements:

HUSBAND RYAN

If I let my wife wander around Brent
On Halloween, dressed like a 'slutty witch',
What does that make me? Basically, her bitch.
That's like building your house on shifting sand;
That's like trying to catch water in your hand;
That's a bloody mug's game, and I'm no mug!

ALVITA

And on and on. And I was just like: ugh.
I didn't listen to a word of it.
Him nagging, his guilt trips, none of it.
I wasn't going to be preached at by him –
I hate anyone tries to rein me in.
Am I alone, ladies? Didn't think so.
If he could have, he'd've killed me, I know,
But by that point, the feeling was mutual.
So, here's the context I need to give you all.
The real reason I tore that page out his book,
And he box mi left ear wid a right hook:
See, he quoted from this book night and day
It was his Bible.

HUSBAND RYAN
       My gospels, I'd say,
Of Saints Farrell, Moxon, Peterson, Strauss –

ALVITA
(Like this was a joke to bring down the house.)

HUSBAND RYAN
It's made of some books I've put together,
Twelve Rules of Life; *The Myth of Male Power*;
The Game; something called *The Woman Racket.*

ALVITA
(Some mental crap he got off the Internet . . .)

HUSBAND RYAN
So then this became my new daily thing:
Whenever I wasn't busy studying
For my Master's –

ALVITA
            – he read this stuff on crap wives.
He knew more about evil women's lives
Than there are saints in the Good News Bible . . . !
Trust me: your average young man is liable
To believe the only true good woman

In this world is his mum or blessed nan!
The rest of us? Witches, out to get him.

ZAIRE
But who wrote all these books about women?
Mate, if women wrote the books he studied
The list of wives abused, misused, bloodied
Would be longer than the Good Book itself!
It'd be too bloody big to fit on the shelf!

ALVITA
What it is, is: Ryan's under the star
Of Mercury. I'm Venus. So we are
Fundamentally incompatible.
Mercury's maths, it's science: rational.
Venus: she loves to party, spend – and dance.
We're so different we never had a chance.
When one of our stars is high in the sky,
The other must fall. That's the reason why
Young sons of Mercury, like my Ryan,
Get all woman-hating and then buy in
To the claim *we're* the problematic ones!
Then, when they're old, and their hard-ons are gone,
These same professors go and write their tomes
On how we should know our place and stay home!
But to get to the point: I'm telling you

How I got smacked for a book. It's all true:
One night Ryan, this Scottish husband of mine,
Was into his book and reading out lines
About wicked women, starting with Eve,
No less, who wrecked the world, Ryan believed:

HUSBAND RYAN
Cos she's to blame for original sin,
And that's why Christ had to be brought in,
And then killed, so we could be forgiven.

ALVITA
Sure: all the fault of one stupid woman!
Then he's on to how:

HUSBAND RYAN
                  Samson lost his hair:
While kipping. His girl sliced it with a pair
Of shears.

ALVITA
Which somehow made him lose his eyes?
But we're not done: next it's ancient Greek guys.

Tearing curtains off the windows to use as togas, the PUB
CHORUS *act out the following scenes:*

He's reading – out loud –

HUSBAND RYAN

about Deianira
Who set her man Hercules on fire.
Then it's poor Socrates, whose wife poured piss
On his head. Xanthippe.

ALVITA

And the weird thing is
The dyam fool just sit there, like a dead man,
And wipe his forehead, and then all he can
Say is:

SOCRATES
After the thunder, comes the rain.

ALVITA
He'd two wives, that fool, and they both caused him pain.
But the story Ryan most liked to repeat
Was really *nasty*. So, the Queen of Crete –
Pasiphaë – for some reason shagged this bull?
And she gave birth to . . . well, like, not a full
Bull, it was a minotaur? Like, half man –
You know what? No. I can't even stand
To say. Then there's this Clytemnestra bitch

Who did the dirty on her man, a sitch
Which led to him dying. Ryan *loved* that.
There was Eriphyle, this girl who, for a fat
Gold chain, sold out her husband, Amphiaraus.
The Greeks demanded to know where he was:

CHORUS OF GREEKS
We suspect he hides somewhere in Thebes!
But where?

ALVITA
And wifey like:

ERIPHYLE
Here. Gold chain, please!

ALVITA
Then on to Livia and Lucilla.
Both of them were stone-cold husband killers.
Liv straight up poisoned hers cos she'd always
Truly hated and dreaded him from day
One. Meanwhile Lucilla's dark devotion
Was so strong she gave her man a love potion
So that he wouldn't chirps no other girls,
But it was toxic – so he left this world.
Point being:

HUSBAND RYAN
   I've read around and I've found
You really can't win if you're a husband.

ALVITA
Then he told me how this Latumius
Was

HUSBAND RYAN
   — bitching to a friend called Arrius
How three of his wives had hung themselves right
In his garden, on a tree, out of spite.

ALVITA
And Arrius is like:

ARRIUS
     Well, listen, mate:
A cutting from that tree would be great,
And I'll plant it in my yard happily!

ALVITA
But it wasn't just old tales he told me.
He read all the latest tabloid nightmares
About husband murderers:

ASMA

                        Who kept their
Husbands' corpses in a cupboard while they
Got hot and heavy with their brand-new bey
In the same room.

ALVITA

                    These stories were hardcore:

The PUB CHORUS *ladies read these headlines from trashy
supermarket tabloids and magazines.*

ZAIRE

Some had put nails through their brains while they snored
And killed them that way.

PUBLICAN POLLY

                        Some had spiked their drinks.

ALVITA

He'd heard them all. I couldn't bear to think
How many. Plus he knew more anti-wife
Online memes than there are seconds in this life.

*We see these memes projected as huge screenshots on the back
wall, texted from* RYAN *to* ALVITA. ZAIRE *reads the cap-
tions out loud and takes us through this presentation.*

ZAIRE
'*Happy wife, happy life*. But nothing rhymes
With *Happy husband*, ever wonder why?
Welcome to married life, dumbass.' That's one.
There's the one with the guy who looks done,
Sitting on the street, tragic-looking fella –
'Saw his face and offered him a dollar:
He said: *I'm not homeless, I'm married!*'
Like a wife is a terminal disease.
Or on a napping Kim K it'll say:
Sleeping Beauty: cute by night, whore by day.

ALVITA
Can you imagine how much it hurt me
To listen to this pure misogyny?
And when I saw him about to restart
Reading that damn book:

We see this vital re-enactment:

ZAIRE

                    She tore it apart,
Tore three pages while he was reading them:

ALVITA

And I'm not the strongest, but there and then
I pulled back my fist and clocked him proper
Hard on his cheek. He fell. Came a cropper
In the fireplace, arse over tit. Then rose
Up, raging like a pitbull, then *he* chose
To get up and strike *me* upside my head.
I hit the floor, and lie down like mi dead.

ZAIRE

And when he saw how very still she lay,
He was bricking it. Almost ran away,
But then she come to and raised up her head.

ALVITA

Rare, you for real tried to kill me!

ZAIRE

                        She said.

ALVITA

You'd kill me for the cash, the Subaru,
This flat? Well, 'fore I die, let me kiss you!

ZAIRE

And he came to her side and knelt right down,
Full of shame and with his heart in his mouth,
He said:

HUSBAND RYAN

      I love you, darling Alvita,
I swear to God I will never beat yer.
Though it was sort of your fault that I did,
I hope you'll find it in your heart to forgive.

ALVITA

So I punched him again, hard with my fist,
And said: 'Listen, teef! Too late, you've missed
Your chance. I'm dying. And done talking to you.'
But as it goes, and after we'd talked it through
A long time, we did manage to agree . . .
That everything would be decided by me:
The flat stayed in my name, and the motor,
Boy can't move without checking my rota.
And now that I run tings completely
You'll hear him say:

HUSBAND RYAN
                    Oh, my amazing wife,
Do whatever you want with your own life;
What's best for you is clearly best for me.

ALVITA
And after that day, we had no more beef.
Lawd, for a kinder wife you couldn't arks
If you searched from India to Denmark.
And to be fair, he's also kind to me.
I pray to God – well, through my Auntie P –
To bless him, seeing as now he submits
To me. Right: my tale. You still up for it?

There is encouraging applause from the PUB AUDIENCE,
*but as it dies down, we hear one loud, somewhat contemptuous
laugh rise above the rest, until it is the only voice left. Everyone,
including* ALVITA, *looks for the source, and finds it is smug*
PASTOR JEGEDE. ALVITA *is unamused.*

ALVITA
Excuse me: did I say something funny?

PASTOR JEGEDE
Oh, sister, I think that was easily
The longest introduction I have heard,
It seemed to be at least eight thousand words!

PASTOR JEGEDE *keeps on laughing and* ALVITA *looks like she's about to go for him, but she's held back by* BARTOSZ, *a beefy-looking Polish man, who steps forward to confront the* PASTOR.

ALVITA (*ASIDE, TO THE AUDIENCE*)
Bartosz. A bailiff. Does what needs doing.

BARTOSZ
I can't believe, for me is amusing:
Why men of church always put nose in
Where don't belong? How I can listen him?
Man of church is like fly. Always he's in,
Everything. Like fly. See he falls in food,
In business, everything! No, is not good.
He says 'long'. But how he is saying long
When he is interrupt? When *he* makes long!
This woman, good woman, she tell story.
Never is boring. No, *he* is boring.

PASTOR JEGEDE
This is your opinion. But I could tell
Some stories about bailiffs and the hell
They put good people through – bailiffs like you –
And we'd laugh, and know who is the buffoon.

BARTOSZ
I am bailiff, yes, but I curse your face!
I am cursing men of church in this place!
Many, many story I can tell from
My country! My story are very strong,
You can say this? Strong? And make shame to you,
And you will not like because story is true!

PUBLICAN POLLY
All right, simmer down: that's enough of that!
Let her get on with . . . what she's getting at.
I'm surprised at you, Father: you two sound
Like two pissheads, brawling. Trust me, around
Here we get enough of that. Alvita?

ALVITA
Always ready to speak verse in meter!
I mean, *if* it's okay with Pastor here . . .

PASTOR JEGEDE
Please, go on with your tale: I am all ears.

THE WIFE OF WILLESDEN'S TALE

FIRST CHILD *walks across the stage – like a scene changer in a medieval revel – holding an enormous sign which reads:*

THE WIFE OF WILLESDEN'S TALE

SECOND CHILD *walks in the opposite direction with an equally large sign:*

> Transferred from Arthurian Camelot
> to Maroon Town, Jamaica

FIRST CHILD *walks by once more with the sign:*

> Featuring Queen Nanny!
> Famed rebel slave and leader of peoples!

As before, ALVITA *tells the story but the* PUB CHORUS *dramatizes it.*

AUNTIE P
Back in the Maroon days of Queen Nanny,
Who Jamaicans love to the *n*th degree

All the island full up ah duppy,*
And all kind ah spirit a roam free . . .
River Mumma hide a golden table
Under her skirts, and Ol' Higue
She suck de breath from de sleeping baby –

ALVITA
At least, that's what my Auntie P told me:
We're talking way back in the seventeen twenties,
Bit before my time. Now'days no one sees
Ghosts or spirits or witches or duppy
Cos the island full up with nuff pastor,
Preachermen, vicar and minister,
Witnesses and Seventh-day Adventists,
Latter-day Saints, Catholics and Baptists,
Who spend their days hunting for evil deeds,
In every field and yard and running stream;
Dash round blessing anyone they can reach,
They're every-damn-where like sand on a beach;
Blessing dance halls, cafes, hotels, high schools,
Nightclubs, hairdresser's, sports grounds, swimming pools.
And why would the spirits wan' deal with that?
Wherever di duppy dem used to be at

---

*A malevolent spirit or ghost. River Mumma and Ol' Higue are both
fearsome female figures from Jamaican folklore.

Now preacherman ah go all round
Praying for your soul, kneeling 'pon de ground,
And asking God to have mercy on us.
Jamaican women these days make no fuss
About fearing duppy; they're too busy
Avoiding these churchmen who wan' weigh she
Down with sin. Anyway: our Queen Nanny
Had a young buck Maroon in her army
Who one day rode to Cudjoe's Leeward Land,
Where he saw a beautiful, young Akan
Girl, early one morning, just walking by,

We see this re-enacted by DARREN *and* KELLY.

A virgin, with no interest in this guy,
But he wouldn't stop.

Pause.

                        He thought his strength gave
Him the right.

Longer pause.

                Well, Cudjoe Town was outraged
By this criminal oppression, and so

Many protested to Captain Cudjoe
That the young Maroon was condemned to death,
By the law courts of St Elizabeth.
Now, that was the sentence of judge and jury –
But Queen Nanny and some Windward ladies
Begged the Captain to

THREE WINDWARD LADIES
                      Tink again and give
This bad young bwoy to us and let him live,
And leave the Leeward, and give Nanny a shot
At deciding whether to kill him or not.

ALVITA
Nanny was glad the King had changed his tune –
The boy came. And she said to this Maroon:

QUEEN NANNY
Yuh nuh outta trouble yet! Mi might still
Kill you. But capital punishment will
Only go so far. I'm interested in
Restorative justice. Understanding
Who you hurt and why. So here is my deal:
You'll live – *if* you can tell me what *we* feel –
I mean we women. What *we* most desire.
You tell me that? I won't set you on fire.

And if you don't have the answer right now
I give you permission to leave this town
A year and a day. Wherever you go
Ask everybody you meet if *they* know.
But before you leave, you must guarantee
That when 'Time's up' you come straight back to me.

ALVITA
This young Maroon was proper screwing
Because suddenly he wasn't doing
Whatever he wanted. He had no choice
But to submit to the powerful voice
Of Queen Nanny, and start on his journey,
Then come back in a year on bended knee,
To this Queen, with an answer that would fly.
So off he rode, feeling very hard done by.
This bwoy went everywhere, to every yard,
Looking for anyone who had thought hard
About

YOUNG MAROON
     Wat women want and love the most,
From the Blue Mountains to town and coast,
Me can't find no one, enslaved or free,
Fi give me answers wat mek wi all agree!

ALVITA
Some said:

Here members of the PUB CHORUS, *as well as some of Alvita's* HUSBANDS, *interject:*

HUSBAND WINSTON
The thing women love most is money.

ALVITA
Some said:

HUSBAND IAN
They're drawn to power like bears to honey!

ALVITA
Some said:

AUNTIE P
Personally, I'm quite fond of jewels . . .

ZAIRE
Women want actual orgasms, you fools!
And to have multiple partners – unjudged.

ALVITA
But some said:

HUSBAND ELRIDGE
       Give me a break. Can we please not fudge
The issue. Admit you're most satisfied
When we worship you with flattering lies!

ALVITA
And you know, if you put the lying part
Aside, it's fair to say we'll give our hearts
To that person who brings us attention,
Takes care of business and, yes, who mentions
The good things about us. But that's just love!
Now, some went proper *deep*. Some said:

*We are surprised to find the women with the deepest thoughts
are people we've hardly noticed up to now:* KELLY, *Alvita's
niece;* PUBLICAN POLLY; *and* ASMA, *the young rebel
wife. They all now stand to speak, and with an intensity that
changes the atmosphere in the pub. They speak in their natural
accents – Black-British Kilburn for* KELLY, *Pakistan-
inflected for* ASMA *– but the words themselves seem to come
from a transnational sacred text of rights and duties. These
women are bearing witness to a truth.*

KELLY

                           Above
All things, we want freedom. Freedom to know
Our own desires. We want to follow
Them where they lead.

ASMA

                     We want to be free from
The bitter critique of men, banging on
And on about our apparent failings.

PUBLICAN POLLY
We want to hear no more of men saying
We have no judgement or reason. We are
Also wise.

ALVITA *breaks the spell of solemnity.*

ALVITA

               Yes, wise enough to know where our
Sore spots are. Where the truth hurts. If you ask
To touch us there, there's a kick up the arse
For telling us the bit we don't want to
Hear or take on board. Come try it and you'll

See. We nuh easy! Not women nor girls.
Still, it's nice to think we're perfect angels . . .
Now, some said:

We see Colin's fiancée SOPHIE, *now dressed like an eighteenth-century British woman on the island, fanning herself from the heat.*

SOPHIE

What we *so* appreciate
Is being considered, as women, great
And loyal friends. Who can keep a secret,
Choose a purpose, and be steadfast to it.
And who never betray a confidence.

ALVITA
Maybe you think that all makes perfect sense,
But we have a saying round here: *Finger
Neber say: 'Look here,' 'im say: 'Look yonder.'*
Meaning: people don't like to point out their
Own flaws? But I know women tell and share
Secrets. If they say they don't they're lying.
'S'like that tale I read in that book of Ryan's
About King Midas – you wanna hear it?

The PUB CHORUS *look at each other and then with slight weariness grab their curtain-togas again for this brief interlude. Throughout the next section,* RYAN *plays King Midas. We may get the sense, as the story progresses, that* ALVITA *is talking less about Midas's dirty secret as much as Ryan's marital failings, principally his domestic abuse, which is a secret, of course, that Alvita has refused to keep . . . And as they tell the apparently frivolous story of Midas, we sense a more serious subtext beneath.*

ALVITA
Won't take a minute: this one's Ovid,
Roman poet. He wrote this likkle ting:
That under Midas's long hair, the King
Had two big ol' donkey ear, which he hid,
Right, because you would. And he truly did
It well. *So* well, that only his own wife
Knew it. And he trusted her with his life.
He begged her:

HUSBAND RYAN
           Tell no one. Never confess
My sad, deforming, secret ugliness.

ALVITA
And she promised she never would. She flat
Out *swore* she would never do him like that.
No, not for the world would she drag his name
Through the streets. Honestly, *she'd* be ashamed.
But then the thing was: it was killing her
To have to keep this secret forever.
She was heart-sick. Like, a physical pain?
What she had to say she couldn't contain
Inside her. And because she didn't dare
Tell no one, she dashed down to this marsh where
Some water was – and, with her heart on fire,
Booming like pub lady at closing hour –
She put her mouth to the water and cried:
'*Water, keep my secret! What I say hide*
Deep within you. But between you and me?
My man him have long ears just like donkey!
Now that's better. I feel calm and at peace.
Couldn't keep that secret no longer, believe.'

At some point during this retelling, RYAN *raises a hand to*
hit ALVITA *again, but she catches it by the wrist, and holds*
it up as a shameful object for the audience to see.

ALVITA
That's it. We can lie and push it all down
Till we just can't. Time's up. Truth gets around.

The melancholy tone suddenly switches, and ALVITA's *back to her playful self.*

For more Midas – if that's your cup of tea –
Go to O, Ovid: Kilburn Library.
Back to this Maroon I was discussing:
When he understood it was not nuffing
To find out what women them love the best
Him heart sunk low in him sorrowful chest.
But it was time: he could put it off no
Longer. He had to face Nanny and go
Home. And on the way back, so sad and stressed,
He found himself in a green wilderness,
Where he saw a whole heap of young gal dem
Dancing on the forest floor, in tandem . . .

We see this dance, as some of the young women of the PUB
CHORUS *get up and do a routine: the Cameo Slide Dance.*
ALVITA *joins them. The scene is lit so as to suggest these girls
might be spirits or apparitions of some kind . . .*

And he started walking towards the dance
Thinking

YOUNG MAROON
I'll ask *these* girls: this is my chance!

ALVITA
But 'fore fi him leg reach, them up and fly.
Completely vanished! Who knows how or why . . .
There wasn't a soul left in that forest
'Cept, on the grass sat an old wife. Honest,
You never see such a muss-muss woman
In your life. Ugly. And she raise her hand
And say:

We see AUNTIE P *dressed up to resemble a foul, troll-like old Obeah woman.*

OLD WIFE
Young bwoy! You c'yannot pass troo here.
But tell me what you seek; speak in my ear,
Maybe it turn out I can help you, man!
Dere's tings only ol' women unnerstan'.

YOUNG MAROON
Oh, Auntie, I'm really struggling, you know?
Truth is, I'm a dead man if I can't show
I know what women want most on this earth.
If you know, I'll pay you . . . whatever works.

OLD WIFE
If *you* will swear that the next ting I ask
You to do, *you will do*. You can't pass,
Or say no. And if these terms be all right
I'll give you your answer before tonight.

YOUNG MAROON
Yes, Auntie. I'll do whatever it is.

OLD WIFE
Then all will be good, young man, I promise.
Your life is safe; I am your guarantee
And I've no doubt Queen Nanny will agree.
Would that lofty woman – who runs tings here,
In her tall headcloth, with her shining spear –
Dare to say no to what *I* come to teach?
But no more talking: let's go so we reach . . .

ALVITA
Then she whispered something in his ear,
She tol' him:

OLD WIFE
　　　Be happy; be free of fear . . .

The pub transforms into QUEEN NANNY*'s stronghold.*

ALVITA
When they reached Nanny's stronghold, this Maroon
Said:

YOUNG MAROON
　　　Promise kept – down to the afternoon!
And I'm ready with my answer for you.

ALVITA
Every woman in Windward had come to
Hear: wives, young servant girls, plenty widow –
All of them wise – and Queen Nanny, yuh know,
Sitting in her throne, eager like the rest.
She chose the hour: the boy came for his test.

QUEEN NANNY
I want silence from each and every one
Of you. I want to hear this young boy run
His mouth.

ALVITA
                    And him nah speak quiet like mouse:
Him open his mouth and bring down de house!

YOUNG MAROON
Queen Nanny, who rules this place with iron fist:
The thing women want is basically this:
They want their husbands to consent, freely;
To *submit to their wives' wills* – which should be
Natural in love; for we submit to love.

Pause.

To keep power, and have no man above
Them – all women want this. And you can kill
Me, but I speak the truth. Do what you will.

ALVITA
And no wife or widow in Nanny Town
Could disagree with how he broke it down.

They all felt he deserved to keep his life.
But soon as she hear, up stands the old wife:

OLD WIFE
Wait now: I found this boy 'pon de grass.
Lawd-a-mercy, Queen Nanny! 'Fore you pass
Out of dis place, I truly, humbly arks
You to do right by me. That is your task.
I gave this answer to the boy. And he
Made a very solemn promise to me:
That if he lived, he'd do what I asked him
To do, no matter what it was. Now, in
Sight of all Windward people: on my life,
Maroon boy, you swore I'd become your wife.
You know *dyam well* I saved your brown backside.
And if I'm lying, tell me how and why.

Now when YOUNG MAROON *speaks, he sounds less like
an eighteenth-century soldier, and more and more like a young
man from The Ends.*

YOUNG MAROON
Oh, mate . . . How is this even happening?
Have you seen yourself? Look, I'm promising
I'll give you something else. Choose anything.
You can take all my creps, my diamond rings,

But please leave my body! *It's my body.*

OLD WIFE
Say this, and a curse falls on you and me!
I may be too old and ugly and poor
But there's nothing in this life I want more
Than to be your wife. Won't swap it for all
The jewels in your ear or creps in your hall.
I mean to be your wife, and even above
That, I mean to be, Maroon boy, your love!

YOUNG MAROON
Your what now? Er, you can't be serious?
I am a Maroon. We're imperious
People: we control our own destinies.
I can't marry a . . . *hag.* Nah, that ain't me.

ALVITA
So *he* said. But it made no difference.
He had to marry her – he'd no defence –
He took his old, poor, muss-muss wife to bed.
Now, some theatre-critic types will say
That I'm lazy and should add to the play
A scene from the wedding. With all the joy
And beautiful outfits the hag and boy
Wore, and the feast, and all that. Let's be clear:

There weren't no joy. Only sadness and fear.
He wed her in total secret, next day.
And all day after that he hid away
Like a mole, from his poor, old muss-muss wife,
Desperate and sad at the state of his life.
He was so cut up about it when he
At last came to bed, he thrashed in the sheets,
While his wife lay there watching all the while.
And she said – while wearing a great big smile –

OLD WIFE
Oh, my likkle husband, blessings to you!
Do all Maroons treat their wives like you do?
Can this be the law in Queen Nanny's land?
Does each Maroon wife have an awful man?
Young'un, I'm your love. I'm also your wife.
I am she that come fi save yer dyam life!
You and I know that I've done right by you.
So how you ah go treat me like me foofool?
Yuh a gwaan like seh yu head nuh good.
Please tell me what I did to you? You should
Explain – Lawd knows – so I can fix it up.

YOUNG MAROON
Listen: you think you didn't stitch me up?
Look at my situation! Tell me how
Any of this can be 'fixed up'? Come on, now.
You're so butters* and old – and honestly?
You're from trash . . . Yeah, you're too ghetto for me!
You think it's weird that I'm thrashing in bed?
Wish my heart would buss up and leave me dead!

OLD WIFE
And that's the only reason you're upset?

YOUNG MAROON
Oh, my days, woman – don't you get it yet?

OLD WIFE
Well, Maroon boy, I could fix all a dat
If I so chose, in about tree days flat,
If you just treat me a likkle bit kind.
But your ideas about good men I find
Ignorant. You think because you born high,
And your family have money, by and by,
That will make you a noble or good man?

---

*Old Weezian term meaning 'unattractive'.

For arrogance like that I got less than
No respect. The proper good man always
Is him who sets himself a goal each day
To do as many good deeds as he can –
That's what I will call a real gentleman.
It's from the likes of Christ we learn kindness,
Not from aristocrats and dey riches.
Cos even if you descended from them
And you got the same high-born fancy name,
You will still inherit nutting at all –
No one does. Just cos your pa act moral
Or your grampa, it don't pass down to you!
No matter how much dey wished that it do.
Some people quote de poets but I like
The wisdom of the yard and the street life,
And there you hear the simple people say:
Ebry day fishing day, but ebry day
*No fe catch fish.** And God mean it that way.
Not all of de men can be good all day.
It's *hard* to be good. And from our elders
We catch nutting but our bodies. Shelter
For a while, till dem frail, and die . . . Yes, sir!
Goodness ain't passed down like your hair colour,
Maroon boy, everybody knows the truth.

---

*Patois: 'Reward does not always follow labour.'

If all it took to be noble was roots
In some old family plot, then these clans
From H'england – with dey grand old posh names and

It might be fun to have a family tree projected somewhere on the back wall, or to have this imagined family otherwise drama-tized on stage.

Sugar wealth – they'd shine, all generations.
But *he* beat his wife. *He* ran plantation.

Pause, as everyone on stage starts to recognize the wisdom of the OLD WIFE, *and gather round her, as round a fire, which fire we now see.*

Imagine I get a burning bush, and I take
It to the darkest house 'tween here and Lake
Victoria. And I just shut the door
And come home. Ya nah see it burn no more
Or less than if twenty thousand men see
It burn? Fire don't need witness to be
Fire. It burn naturally then it go
Out. Will looking at it change it? Lawd, no.
So do you see how goodness in a man
Got nutting to do with who's in his clan?

People act like dey gonna act, like fire.
Can't make dem do as you yourself desire.
No matter the posh names they've been given,
Sons of high-born often turn out villain.

Now, as ALVITA *speaks, we see the* OLD WIFE, *agreeing
and supporting her, thankful for her intervention.* ALVITA
*speaks to the real theatre audience, and perhaps comes out to
walk amongst them.*

ALVITA
There's probably a few of you who are feeling
Yourselves, because you're old money, reeling
It in; and you're called Rees-Mogg or what have
You: Don't you know you can still be a chav
In your soul? What have you done? Not a thing.
Depend on your family for everything.
Maybe your grandad was someone. Maybe
Your mum. What have you actually achieved?
Nowt. An old name doesn't make you classy,
That won't cut it, nor your daddy's money,
Real class is a gift from God. It's pure grace.
It don't come from Eton or that other place.
Think about how noble Marley himself
Was. Him rise from poverty to great wealth,

But it was his ideas that made him kind
And good: *None but ourselves can free our minds.**

OLD WIFE
Dear husband, I must say it seems to me –
Even though my people are poor, country
Folk – I might be able to live a good
Life, God-willing, and do the things I should.
I'll call myself good only when I start
Switching sinfulness for good in my heart.
And when you cuss me for being so poor –
Who wore just sandals and asked for no more?
In radical poverty he lived life
And surely any man, young gal, or wife
Will understand what was good enough
For a poor Nazareth boy is sure nuff
Good enough for me. No shame in being
Poor. Or satisfied with enough. Seeing
Them fools who wan be rich above all things –
But never can be? Those men *suffering*.
But the man who say *enough* is content,
Even if he has no shirt. That man want
Nothing. He is wealthy in his own soul.
Even if you call him a criminal.

---

*Bob Marley actually borrowed this line from Marcus Garvey.

ALVITA

True poverty sings, in reality!

At this point a small circle of GOSPEL SINGERS, *who sit at the table with* PASTOR JEGEDE, *stand up and begin singing the refrain 'True poverty sings, in reality' in a Gospel style. At first it seems beautiful – a renouncing of the logic of capital, in which a person's worth is determined by their wealth. But as* PASTOR JEGEDE *– who we might notice looks conspicuously wealthy, with many gold rings and chains – stands on a table to give his smug homily, and* CHURCH USHERS *move around the Colin Campbell with plates, collecting money from variously willing people,* ALVITA *– and the audience – begins to suspect that the radical vision of Christ is being transformed into something else entirely.* ALVITA, *we notice, refuses point-blank to put money on the plate, and the next thing she says is said with a certain irony:*

ALVITA

And Pastor speaks of it *so* pos'tively:

PASTOR JEGEDE

One great blessing of poverty is when
A thief comes near a poor man, well, then,
That poor man has no reason to worry.
No thief comes to *his* door! He'll be merry!

Yes, in some ways it's awful, poverty.
But it's motivating! Keeps you busy.
It can be very educational
Especially if you are rational
And patient in accepting it. It may
Seem miserable. But at least you can say:
'Poverty's mine: you can't take it from me!
I'm perfectly poor, and poor perfectly!'
And often poverty brings you so low
It actually brings you to God! Also,
You'll find out a lot about the real you.
It's like a mirror – I find this so true –
In which you find out who your real friends are.

The collection finished, PASTOR JEGEDE *steps down from
his pulpit. He notices the* OLD WIFE *waiting for a blessing,
and gives her a cursory one – though he seems more interested
in the plate that is being returned to him and which he now
smoothly empties into his pockets, before sitting back down,
satisfied. The* OLD WIFE *looks unsure of his sermon – and
the sincerity of his blessing – but shrugs and decides to use its
dubious message for her own purposes.*

OLD WIFE
As you've heard, I've done nothing to you, sir!
Even if I'm poor, I won't let you scold

Me for it. Now, you blame me cos I'm old.
I can't find where it says it in the books,
But I know polite people say when you look
'Pon an ol' man, try to be kind with him.
Say: 'sir' or 'uncle' – show respect to him.
And them who write books say the same, I guess . . .
You say I'm old and ugly. But confess
That means you don't need to worry I cheat.
Cos being poor and ugly is a sweet
Way to keep a person faithful always
Until the bitter end of both of your days.
But I've seen: you're basic. You've had your say:
For *you* looks matter. Okay. Have your way.
But choose now. Which one of these will you try:
To have me old and ugly till I die
And be a dedicated, loving wife
Who will please you all the days of your life?
Or you can have me younger and pretty
But take the risk, when we're up in the city,
That every handsome young bwoy wan kiss me,
Here, there, and places you c'yant even see!
The choice is yours: you must do as you feel.

ALVITA
And the boy thought deeply: he stressed and sighed,
Then he turned to his old wife and replied:

YOUNG MAROON
You know what? You're my girl, my wife, my love,
You blatantly know a lot about stuff.
I'll put myself in your hands – you decide.
Choose the best thing, or what makes you feel pride
In both of us. I'm easy. You do you.
If you're into it, I'm, like, on board, too . . .

We see the OLD WIFE *tying a silk scarf around his eyes, a blindfold, which seems like it might be borrowed from someone's boudoir. She ties his hands behind his back with another silk scarf. And then changes places with* ALVITA, *who takes it from here, while the* YOUNG MAROON *becomes more obviously* DARREN. *We hear Chaka Khan's 'I'm Every Woman' playing. The next scene between* ALVITA *and* DARREN *feels very intimate, like an erotic scene from their real life.*

ALVITA
So now you agree: I am the master?
I'm in control? Not *ask him* but *ask her?*

HUSBAND DARREN
Yes, my wife, I know now that you know best.

ALVITA

Kiss me, bwoy . . . No more fighting, no more stress.
I swear I'll be every woman to you:
Fit and good and smart and true.
I swear to God I'd rather die crazy
Than be anything but the best lady
Wife this world ever saw. I'll be so good
To you, baby. And in a sec you should
See before you the fittest, finest Fly
Gal you ever seen. Beyoncé look dry
Next to me. Jourdan Dunn an old skinny
Bird next to me. I outshine Naomi.
And if you discover I tell a lie
My life is yours: I'm not afraid to die.
Now let me take this off so you can see
This make-over that has come over me!

ALVITA *pulls off the blindfold to reveal her fabulous, thick,
middle-aged beauteousness. And* DARREN *looks delighted,
though some of* ALVITA*'s descriptions of what happens next
seem almost like magical commands that impel him to act as
she says he did.*

ALVITA
Yes, man. When the young boy saw all of *this*,
How young she was and how totally fit,
He hug her up tight-tight in his big arms.
His heart was so uplifted by her charms.
He was all over her . . . simply obsessed . . .

*ALVITA pauses in her narrative for a gratuitous kiss of panto-
mime length.*

He submitted – and she was his the rest
Of the time. Did the sorts of things he liked
And brought nothing but pleasure to their life.
And that's how they spent their lives together.
Hashtag *blessed*. Oh, Lawd Jesus Christ, forever
Send us meek, young husbands who are good in bed
And let us long outlive the men we wed!
And as for those wastemen who won't be ruled
By their wives, I pray the Lord makes those fools'
Lives short. All those old, angry, stingy men.
May you be cussed down high road and back again!

The CROWD *in the Colin Campbell give a great cheer – and
hopefully the real audience, too.*

*The stereo comes back on, the pub reverts to a normal night,
everybody talking, laughing, drinking.* ALVITA *is dancing
with all her* HUSBANDS, *dead and alive . . . The scene seems
about to fade out, but the* AUTHOR *makes her way through
the crowd to give her retraction.*

A RETRACTION

AUTHOR

So, yeah . . . No more couplets . . . That shit's *exhausting* to write . . . No, I'm just taking my leave of you . . . Chaucer called this bit the Retraction . . . and I just want to say I hope you had a good time, but if you didn't, listen: blame me . . . And all credit to Chaucer if you liked it – he's the source of all the actual wisdom . . . But, look, on the other hand, if it annoyed or offended you in some way, that's just a lack of finesse on my part, probably . . . so don't blame Chaucer . . . I take full responsibility . . . and while I'm here, back in The Ends, I might as well offer a broader sort of apologia to Brent, as a whole? So: sorry for all the swearing and cultural appropriation in my first book . . .

As this retraction is made, we see different bits of the apology directed at different characters – all of whom are busy dancing or drinking or celebrating – and who either pay no notice or take the apologies directed at them in a variety of ways. The swearing apology is directed at ALVITA*'s religious relatives – though* AUNTIE P *is entirely unmoved by it – while* ZAIRE *basically accepts the sex apology.* ASMA *and* BARTOSZ *hear her out on the cultural appropriation, although with some scepticism, and so on . . .*

And a bit more cultural appropriation and heresy in the second . . . and the dodgy sex in the third; um . . . the existential bleakness of the fourth . . . er . . . I could go on—

ALVITA
Hush up! Dance!

AUTHOR
Basically, forgive me, Brent! Have mercy on me!

The AUTHOR *joins* ALVITA *in a how-low-can-you-go dance-off as the lights fade, and the scene ends . . .*

FROM *THE CANTERBURY TALES*

BY GEOFFREY CHAUCER

The Wife of Bath's Prologue

The Wife of Bath's Tale

Chaucer's Retraction

The Wife of Bath's Prologue

"Experience, though noon auctoritee
Were in this world, is right ynogh for me
To speke of wo that is in mariage;
For, lordynges, sith I twelve yeer was of age,
Thonked be God that is eterne on lyve,   5
Housbondes at chirche dore I have had fyve—
If I so ofte myghte have ywedded bee—
And alle were worthy men in hir degree.
But me was toold, certeyn, nat longe agoon is,
That sith that Crist ne wente nevere but onis
To weddyng, in the Cane of Galilee,   11
That by the same ensample taughte he me
That I ne sholde wedded be but ones.
Herkne eek, lo, which a sharp word for the
          nones,

1 **auctoritee:** written authority
10 **onis:** once
11 **Cane:** the town of Cana
14 **Herkne:** listen

Biside a welle, Jhesus, God and man,   15
Spak in repreeve of the Samaritan:
'Thou hast yhad fyve housbondes,' quod he,
'And that ilke man that now hath thee
Is noght thyn housbonde,' thus seyde he cer-
          teyn.
What that he mente therby, I kan nat seyn;   20
But that I axe, why that the fifthe man
Was noon housbonde to the Samaritan?
How manye myghte she have in mariage?
Yet herde I nevere tellen in myn age
Upon this nombre diffinicioun.   25
Men may devyne and glosen, up and doun,
But wel I woot, expres, withoute lye,
God bad us for to wexe and multiplye;
That gentil text kan I wel understonde.
Eek wel I woot, he seyde myn housbonde   30
Sholde lete fader and mooder and take to me.
But of no nombre mencion made he,
Of bigamye, or of octogamye;

16 **repreeve:** reproof
21 **axe:** ask
26 **devyne:** conjecture   **glosen, up and doun:** interpret in every way
27 **expres:** clearly
28 **wexe:** increase (breed)
31 **lete:** leave
33 **octogamye:** marrying eight times

Why sholde men thanne speke of it vileynye?
   Lo, heere the wise kyng, daun Salomon;   35
I trowe he hadde wyves mo than oon.
As wolde God it leveful were unto me
To be rcfresshed half so ofte as he!
Which yifte of God hadde he for alle his
      wyvys!
No man hath swich that in this world alyve is.
God woot, this noble kyng, as to my wit,   41
The firste nyght had many a myrie fit
With ech of hem, so wel was hym on lyve.
Yblessed be God that I have wedded fyve!
[Of whiche I have pyked out the beste,   44a
Bothe of here nether purs and of here cheste.
Diverse scales maken parfyt clerkes,
And diverse practyk in many sondry werkes
Maketh the werkman parfyt sekirly;
Of fyve husbondes scoleiyng am I.]   44f
Welcome the sixte, whan that evere he shal.

34 **vileynye:** in reproach
35 **daun:** sir **Salomon:** Solomon
37 **leveful:** lawful, permissible
39 **Which yifte:** what a gift
41 **wit:** judgment
44b **nether:** lower
44d **practyk:** practice
44e **sekirly:** certainly
44f **scoleiyng:** schooling

For sothe, I wol nat kepe me chaast in al.　　46
Whan myn housbonde is fro the world ygon,
Som Cristen man shal wedde me anon,
For thanne th'apostle seith that I am free
To wedde, a Goddes half, where it liketh me.
He seith that to be wedded is no synne;　　51
Bet is to be wedded than to brynne.
What rekketh me, thogh folk seye vileynye
Of shrewed Lameth and his bigamye?
I woot wel Abraham was an hooly man,　　55
And Jacob eek, as forforth as I kan;
And ech of hem hackle wyves mo than two,
And many another holy man also.
Wher can ye seye, in any manere age,
That hye God defended mariage　　60
By expres word? I pray yow, telleth me.
Or where comanded he virginitee?
I woot as wel as ye, it is no drede,

46 **chaast:** chaste
49 **th'apostle:** St Paul
50 **a Goddes half:** by God's side, by God
52 **brynne:** burn
53 **rekketh me:** do I care
54 **shrewed:** cursed, evil　**Lameth:** the biblical Lamech, the first bigamist
55–56 **Abraham, Jacob:** the biblical patriarchs
61 **expres:** explicit
63 **drede:** doubt

Th' apostel, whan he speketh of maydenhede,
He seyde that precept therof hadde he noon.
Men may conseille a womman to been oon,   66
But conseillyng is no comandement.
He putte it in oure owene juggement;
For hadde God comanded maydenhede,
Thanne hadde he dampned weddyng with the
      dede.
And certes, if ther were no seed ysowe,   71
Virginitee, thanne wherof sholde it growe?
Poul dorste nat comanden, atte leeste,
A thyng of which his maister yaf noon heeste.
The dart is set up for virginitee;   75
Cacche whoso may, who renneth best lat see.
   But this word is nat taken of every wight,
But ther as God lust gyve it of his myght.
I woot wel that th'apostel was a mayde;   79
But nathelees, thogh that he wroot and sayde
He wolde that every wight were swich as he,

---

64 **Th'apostel:** St Paul
73 **Poul:** St Paul
74 **of which his maister yaf noon heeste:** about which his Master made no commandment
75 **dart:** dare offered as a prize
76 **Cacche whoso may:** catch it whoever can
77 **is nat taken of:** does not apply to
78 **lust:** pleases
79 **mayde:** virgin, without sexual experience

Al nys but conseil to virginitee.
And for to been a wyf he yaf me leve
Of indulgence; so nys it no repreve
To wedde me, if that my make dye,   85
Withouten excepcion of bigamye.
Al were it good no womman for to touche—
He mente as in his bed or in his couche,
For peril is bothe fyr and tow t'assemble;
Ye knowe what this ensample may resemble.
This is al and som: he heeld virginitee   91
Moore parfit than weddyng in freletee.
Freletee clepe I, but if that he and she
Wolde leden al hir lyf in chastitee.

I graunte it wel; I have noon envie,   95
Thogh maydenhede preferre bigamye.
It liketh hem to be clene, body and goost;
Of myn estaat I nyl nat make no boost,

82 **Al nys but:** although it is only
84 **Of indulgence:** by permission   **repreve:** shame
85 **make:** mate
86 **excepcion of:** objection on the grounds of
89 **tow:** flax
91 **al and som:** the entire matter
92 **in freletee:** because of weakness
93 **but if that:** unless
94 **chastitee:** abstinence from sexual intercourse
96 **preferre:** may have precedence over   **bigamye:** in this instance, marriage by or with
     a widower or widow
98 **nyl** = *ne wyl*, will not

For wel ye knowe, a lord in his houshold,
He nath nat every vessel al of gold;   100
Somme been of tree, and doon hir lord servyse.
God clepeth folk to hym in sondry wyse,
And everich hath of God a propre yifte—
Som this, som that, as hym liketh shifte.

    Virginitee is greet perfeccion,   105
And continence eek with devocion,
But Crist, that of perfeccion is welle,
Bad nat every wight he sholde go selle
Al that he hadde, and gyve it to the poore,
And in swich wise folwe hym and his foore.
He spak to hem that wolde lyve parfitly;   111
And lordynges, by youre leve, that am nat I.
I wol bistowe the flour of al myn age
In the actes and in fruyt of mariage.

    Telle me also, to what conclusion   115
Were membres maad of generacion,
And of so parfit wys a [wright] ywroght?

101 **of tree:** made of wood
103 **propre yifte:** special, individual gift
104 **hym liketh shifte:** it pleases God to provide
110 **foore:** footsteps
111 **parfitly:** perfectly
115 **conclusion:** purpose
117 And made by so perfectly wise a maker

Trusteth right wel, they were nat maad for
      noght.
Glose whoso wole, and seye bothe up and doun
That they were maked for purgacioun   120
Of uryne, and oure bothe thynges smale
Were eek to knowe a femele from a male,
And for noon oother cause—say ye no?
The experience woot wel it is noght so.
So that the clerkes be nat with me wrothe,   125
I sey this: that they maked ben for bothe;
That is to seye, for office and for ese
Of engendrure, ther we nat God displese.
Why sholde men elles in hir bookes sette
That man shal yelde to his wyf hire dette?   130
Now wherwith sholde he make his paiement,
If he ne used his sely instrument?
Thanne were they maad upon a creature
To purge uryne, and eek for engendrure.   134
    But I seye noght that every wight is holde,

---

119 **Glose:** interpret scripture **up and doun:** in all respects
125 **So that:** providing that
127 **office:** function (of excretion) **ese:** pleasure
128 **engendrure:** procreation
130 **yelde:** pay **dette:** marital debt (obligation to engage in intercourse)
132 **sely instrument:** blessed, innocent tool
135 **holde:** obligated

That hath swich harneys as I to yow tolde,
To goon and usen hem in engendrure.
Thanne sholde men take of chastitee no cure.
Crist was a mayde and shapen as a man,
And many a seint, sith that the world bigan;
Yet lyved they evere in parfit chastitee.　　　141
I nyl envye no virginitee.
Lat hem be breed of pured whete-seed,
And lat us wyves hoten barly-breed;
And yet with barly-breed, Mark telle kan,　　　145
Oure Lord Jhesu refresshed many a man.
In swich estaat as God hath cleped us
I wol persevere; I nam nat precius.
In wyfhod I wol use myn instrument
As frely as my Makere hath it sent.　　　150
If I be daungerous, God yeve me sorwe!
Myn housbonde shal it have bothe eve and
　　　morwe,
Whan that hym list come forth and paye his
　　　dette.

---

143 **pured:** refined
144 **hoten:** be called   **barly-breed:** an inexpensive bread
148 **precius:** fussy, fastidious
151 **daungerous:** grudging

An housbonde I wol have—I wol nat lette—
Which shal be bothe my dettour and my thral,
And have his tribulacion withal   156
Upon his flessh, whil that I am his wyf.
I have the power durynge al my lyf
Upon his propre body, and noght he.
Right thus the Apostel tolde it unto me,   160
And bad oure housbondes for to love us weel.
Al this sentence me liketh every deel"—

   Up stirte the Pardoner, and that anon;
"Now, dame," quod he, "by God and by Seint
      John!
Ye been a noble prechour in this cas.   165
I was aboute to wedde a wyf; allas!
What sholde I bye it on my flessh so deere?
Yet hadde I levere wedde no wyf to-yeere!"

   "Abyde!" quod she, "my tale is nat bigonne.
Nay, thou shalt drynken of another tonne,   170
Er that I go, shal savoure wors than ale.

154 **lette:** leave off, desist
155 **thral:** servant, slave
156 **withal:** also
165 **prechour:** preacher
167 **What:** why **bye it on:** pay for it with
168 **to-yeere:** this year
170 **tonne:** barrel
171 **savoure:** taste

And whan that I have toold thee forth my tale
Of tribulacion in mariage,
Of which I am expert in al myn age—   174
This is to seyn, myself have been the whippe—
Than maystow chese wheither thou wolt sippe
Of thilke tonne that I shal abroche.
Be war of it, er thou to ny approche;
For I shal telle ensamples mo than ten.
'Whoso that nyl be war by othere men,   180
By hym shul othere men corrected be.'
The same wordes writeth Ptholomee;
Rede in his Almageste, and take it there."

   "Dame, I wolde praye yow, if youre wyl it
      were,"
Seyde this Pardoner, "as ye bigan,   185
Telle forth youre tale, spareth for no man,
And teche us yonge men of youre praktike."

   "Gladly," quod she, "sith it may yow like;
But yet I praye to al this compaignye,

---

177 **abroche:** open
178 **to ny:** too close
180–81 He who will not (*nyl* = *ne wyll*) be admonished by examples offered by others must
    himself become an example for the correction of others.
182 **Ptholomee:** Ptolemy, the Greek mathematician and astronomer, author of the *Almageste*
187 **praktike:** practice

If that I speke after my fantasye,   190
As taketh not agrief of that I seye,
For myn entente nys but for to pleye.
   Now, sire, now wol I telle forth my tale.
As evere moote I drynken wyn or ale,   194
I shal seye sooth; tho housbondes that I hadde,
As thre of hem were goode, and two were
            badde.
The thre were goode men, and riche, and olde;
Unnethe myghte they the statut holde
In which that they were bounden unto me.
Ye woot wel what I meene of this, pardee!   200
As help me God, I laughe whan I thynke
How pitously a-nyght I made hem swynke!
And, by my fey, I tolde of it no stoor.
They had me yeven hir lond and hir tresoor;
Me neded nat do lenger diligence   205
To wynne hir love, or doon hem reverence.
They loved me so wel, by God above,
That I ne tolde no deyntee of hir love!

---

190 **after my fantasye:** according to my fancy, desire
191 **As taketh not agrief of:** do not be annoyed with (*as* is not translated)
198 **Unnethe:** hardly   **statut:** the conjugal debt (see 130 above)
202 **a-nyght:** at night   **swynke:** work
203 **fey:** faith   **tolde of it no stoor:** set no store by it, regarded it as useless
204 **tresoor:** treasure
208 **ne tolde no deyntee of:** did not value, reckoned little of

A wys womman wol bisye hire evere in oon
To gete hire love, ye, ther as she hath noon.
But sith I hadde hem hoolly in myn hond,   211
And sith they hadde me yeven al hir lond,
What sholde I taken keep hem for to plese,
But it were for my profit and myn ese?
I sette hem so a-werke, by my fey,   225
That many a nyght they songen 'Weilawey!'
The bacon was nat fet for hem, I trowe,
That som men han in Essex at Dunmowe.
I governed hem so wel, after my lawe,
That ech of hem ful blisful was and fawe   220
To brynge me gaye thynges fro the fayre.
They were ful glad whan I spak to hem faire,
For, God it woot, I chidde hem spitously.

   Now herkneth hou I baar me proprely,
Ye wise wyves, that kan understonde.   225
Thus shulde ye speke and bere hem wrong
           on honde,

---

209 **bisye hire evere in oon:** be constantly busy
213 **taken keep:** take care
215 **sette hem so a-werke:** worked them so hard (or, tricked them)
217–18 **bacon . . . in Essex at Dunmowe:** side of bacon awarded to spouses who lived a
         year and a day without quarrelling
220 **fawe:** eager
223 **chidde hem spitously:** chided, scolded them cruelly
226 **bere hem wrong on honde:** accuse them wrongfully

For half so boldely kan ther no man
Swere and lyen, as a womman kan.
I sey nat this by wyves that been wyse,
But if it be whan they hem mysavyse.   230
A wys wyf, if that she kan hir good,
Shal beren hym on honde the cow is wood,
And take witnesse of hir owene mayde
Of hir assent. But herkneth how I sayde:

'Sire olde kaynard, is this thyn array?   235
Why is my neighebores wyf so gay?
She is honoured overal ther she gooth;
I sitte at hoom; I have no thrifty clooth.
What dostow at my neighebores hous?
Is she so fair? Artow so amorous?   240
What rowne ye with oure mayde? Benedicite!
Sire olde lecchour, lat thy japes be!
And if I have a gossib or a freend,

229 **by:** concerning, about
231 **kan hir good:** knows what's good for her
232 **beren hym on honde:** deceive him by swearing   **cow:** chough, a crow-like bird, which can talk
234 **Of hir assent:** of her agreement (i.e., the maid agrees with what she says)
235 **kaynard:** dotard
237 **overal ther:** wherever
238 **thrifty clooth:** serviceable clothing
241 **rowne:** whisper
243 **gossib:** close friend

Withouten gilt, thou chidest as a feend,
If that I walke or pleye unto his hous!   245
Thou comest hoom as dronken as a mous,
And prechest on thy bench, with yvel preef!
Thou seist to me it is a greet meschief
To wedde a povre womman, for costage;
And if that she be riche, of heigh parage,   250
Thanne seistow that it is a tormentrie
To soffre hire pride and hire malencolie.
And if that she be fair, thou verray knave,
Thou seyst that every holour wol hire have;
She may no while in chastitee abyde,   255
That is assailled upon ech a syde.

    Thou seyst som folk desiren us for richesse,
Somme for oure shap, and somme for oure fair-
      nesse,
And som for she kan outher synge or daunce,
And som for gentillesse and daliaunce;   260

244 **chidest as:** scold like
247 **with yvel preef:** bad luck to you
249 **costage:** expense
250 **heigh parage:** high birth
251 **tormentrie:** torture
252 **malencolie:** anger, sullenness (due to an excess of the humor)
254 **holour:** lecher
256 **ech a:** every
260 **daliaunce:** socializing

Som for hir handes and hir armes smale;
Thus goth al to the devel, by thy tale.
Thou seyst men may nat kepe a castel wal,
It may so longe assailled been overal.

    And if that she be foul, thou seist that she
Coveiteth every man that she may se,   266
For as a spanyel she wol on hym lepe,
Til that she fynde som man hire to chepe.
Ne noon so grey goos gooth ther in the lake
As, seistow, wol been withoute make.   270
And seyst it is an hard thyng for to welde
A thyng that no man wole, his thankes, helde.
Thus seistow, lorel, whan thow goost to bedde,
And that no wys man nedeth for to wedde,
Ne no man that entendeth unto hevene.   275
With wilde thonder-dynt and firy levene
Moote thy welked nekke be tobroke!

261 **smale:** slender
262 **by thy tale:** according to what you say
268 **chepe:** buy (i.e., take)
270 **make:** mate
271 **weld:** control
272 **his thankes:** willingly   **helde:** holde
273 **lorel:** scoundrel
275 **entendeth unto:** hopes (to go) to
276 **thonder-dynt:** thunderstroke   **levene:** lightning
277 **welked:** withered   **tobroke:** broken to pieces

Thow seyst that droppyng houses, and eek
    smoke,
And chidyng wyves maken men to flee
Out of hir owene houses; a, benedicitee!   280
What eyleth swich an old man for to chide?
    Thow seyst we wyves wol oure vices hide
Til we be fast, and thanne we wol hem shewe—
Wel may that be a proverbe of a shrewe!
    Thou seist that oxen, asses, hors, and houndes,
They been assayed at diverse stoundes;   286
Bacyns, lavours, er that men hem bye,
Spoones and stooles, and al swich housbondrye,
And so been pottes, clothes, and array;
But folk of wyves maken noon assay,   290
Til they be wedded—olde dotard shrewe!—
And thanne, seistow, we wol oure vices shewe.
    Thou seist also that it displeseth me

---

278 **droppyng:** dripping, leaky
279 **chidyng:** scolding
283 **fast:** securely tied (in marriage)
284 **shrewe:** scoundrel
286 **diverse stoundes:** different times
287 **Bacyns:** basins **lavours:** wash bowls **bye:** pay for, buy
288 **housbondrye:** household equipment
290 **assay:** trial
291 **dotard shrewe:** senile scoundrel

But if that thou wolt preyse my beautee,
And but thou poure alwey upon my face,   295
And clepe me "faire dame" in every place.
And but thou make a feeste on thilke day
That I was born, and make me fressh and gay;
And but thou do to my norice honour,
And to my chamberere withinne my bour,   300
And to my fadres folk and his allyes—
Thus seistow, olde barel-ful of lyes!

   And yet of oure apprentice Janekyn,
For his crispe heer, shynynge as gold so fyn,
And for he squiereth me bothe up and doun,
Yet hastow caught a fals suspecioun.   306
I wol hym noght, thogh thou were deed to-
      morwe!

   But tel me this: why hydestow, with sorwe,
The keyes of thy cheste awey fro me?
It is my good as wel as thyn, pardee!   310
What, wenestow make an ydiot of oure dame?

---

295 **poure:** gaze intently
299 **norice:** nurse
300 **chamberere:** chambermaid   **bour:** bedchamber
301 **allyes:** kinsmen
302 **lyes:** lees (dregs)
304 **crispe:** curly
305 **squiereth:** formally attends
308 **hydestow:** do you hide   **with sorwe:** bad luck to you
311 **wenestow:** do you expect   **oure dame:** the lady of our house (me)

Now by that lord that called is Seint Jame,
Thou shalt nat bothe, thogh that thou were
    wood,
Be maister of my body and of my good;   314
That oon thou shalt forgo, maugree thyne yen.
What helpith it of me to enquere or spyen?
I trowe thou woldest loke me in thy chiste!
Thou sholdest seye, "Wyf, go wher thee liste;
Taak youre disport; I wol nat leve no talys.
I knowe yow for a trewe wyf, dame Alys."
We love no man that taketh kep or charge   321
Wher that we goon; we wol ben at oure large.

    Of alle men yblessed moot he be,
The wise astrologien, Daun Ptholome,
That seith this proverbe in his Almageste: 325
"Of alle men his wysdom is the hyeste
That rekketh nevere who hath the world in
    honde."
By this proverbe thou shalt understonde,
Have thou ynogh, what thar thee recche or
    care

312 **Seint Jame:** St James of Compostella
317 **loke:** lock **chiste:** strongbox, coffer
319 **leve:** believe
322 **at oure large:** free to act as we wish
327 **in honde:** in his control

How myrily that othere folkes fare?   330
For, certeyn, olde dotard, by youre leve,
Ye shul have queynte right ynogh at eve.
He is to greet a nygard that wolde werne
A man to lighte a candle at his lanterne;
He shal have never the lasse light, pardee.   335
Have thou ynogh, thee thar nat pleyne thee.

    Thou seyst also, that if we make us gay
With clothyng, and with precious array,
That it is peril of oure chastitee;   339
And yet—with sorwe!—thou most enforce
       thee,
And seye thise wordes in the Apostles name:
"In habit maad with chastitee and shame
Ye wommen shul apparaille yow," quod he,
"And noght in tressed heer and gay perree,
As perles, ne with gold, ne clothes riche."   345
After thy text, ne after thy rubriche,

---

331 **dotard:** senile fool
332 **queynte:** my elegant, pleasing thing (sexual favors)
333 **werne:** refuse
336 **thar nat pleyne thee:** need not complain
340 **enforce thee:** make an effort
341 **Apostles:** St Paul's
342 **habit:** clothing
343 **apparaille yow:** dress yourselves
344 **tressed heer:** carefully arranged hair   **perree:** precious stones
346 **rubriche:** words written in red as a heading to a text

I wol nat wirche as muchel as a gnat.

Thou seydest this, that I was lyk a cat;
For whoso wolde senge a cattes skyn,   349
Thanne wolde the cat wel dwellen in his in;
And if the cattes skyn be slyk and gay,
She wol nat dwelle in house half a day,
But forth she wole, er any day be dawed,
To shewe hir skyn and goon a-caterwawed.
This is to seye, if I be gay, sire shrewe,   355
I wol renne out my borel for to shewe.

Sire olde fool, what helpeth thee to spyen?
Thogh thou preye Argus with his hundred yen
To be my warde-cors, as he kan best,
In feith, he shal nat kepe me but me lest;   360
Yet koude I make his berd, so moot I thee!

Thou seydest eek that ther been thynges thre,
The whiche thynges troublen al this erthe,
And that no wight may endure the ferthe.

---

349 **senge:** singe
350 **wolde the cat:** the cat would want   **dwellen:** remain   **his in:** his dwelling-place
351 **slyk:** sleek, shining
353 **dawed:** dawned
354 **a-caterwawed:** caterwauling
356 **borel:** coarse, poor cloth (of which my clothes are made)
358 **Argus:** the mythical guardian of Io, one of Zeus's loves
359 **warde-cors:** bodyguard
361 **make his berd:** deceive him   **so moot I thee:** as I may prosper

O leeve sire shrewe, Jhesu shorte thy lyf!   365
Yet prechestow and seyst an hateful wyf
Yrekened is for oon of thise meschances.
Been ther none othere maner resemblances
That ye may likne youre parables to,
But if a sely wyf be oon of tho?   370
    Thou liknest eek wommenes love to helle,
To bareyne lond, ther water may nat dwelle.
Thou liknest it also to wilde fyr;
The moore it brenneth, the moore it hath desir
To consume every thyng that brent wole be.
Thou seyest, right as wormes shende a tree,   376
Right so a wyf destroyeth hire housbonde;
This knowe they that been to wyves bonde.'
    Lordynges, right thus, as ye have under-
        stonde,
Baar I stifly myne olde housbondes on honed
That thus they seyden in hir dronkenesse;   381
And al was fals, but that I took witnesse
On Janekyn, and on my nece also.
O Lord! The peyne I dide hem and the wo,

373 **wilde fyr:** Greek fire, an inflammable mixture, used in warfare
376 **shende:** destroy
378 **bonde:** bound
380 **Baar I stifly ... on honde:** I firmly swore
382 **but that:** except that
383 **nece:** kinswoman

Ful giltelees, by Goddes sweete pyne!   385
For as an hors I koude byte and whyne.
I koude pleyne, and yit was in the gilt,
Or elles often tyme hadde I been spilt.
Whoso that first to mille comth, first grynt;
I pleyned first, so was oure werre ystynt.   390
They were ful glade to excuse hem blyve
Of thyng of which they nevere agilte hir lyve.
Of wenches wolde I beren hem on honde,
Whan that for syk unnethes myghte they stonde.

   Yet tikled I his herte, for that he   395
Wende that I hadde of hym so greet chiertee!
I swoor that al my walkynge out by nyghte
Was for t'espye wenches that he dighte;
Under that colour hadde I many a myrthe.   399
For al swich wit is yeven us in oure byrthe;

385 **pyne:** suffering
386 **whyne:** whinny, whine
387 **in the gilt:** in the wrong
388 **spilt:** ruined
389 **grynt** = *gryndeth*, grinds
391 **blyve:** quickly
392 **agilte hir lyve:** been guilty in their lives
393 **beren hem on honde:** accuse them
394 **syk:** illness **unnethes:** hardly
395 **tikled:** tickled, pleased
396 **chiertee:** fondness
398 **dighte:** copulated with
399 **colour:** pretense

Deceite, wepyng, spynnyng God hath yive
To wommen kyndely, whil that they may lyve.
And thus of o thyng I avaunte me:
Atte ende I hadde the bettre in ech degree,
By sleighte, or force, or by som maner thyng,
As by continueel murmur or grucchyng.   406
Namely abedde hadden they meschaunce:
Ther wolde I chide and do hem no plesaunce;
I wolde no lenger in the bed abyde,
If that I felte his arm over my syde,   410
Til he had maad his raunson unto me;
Thanne wolde I suffre hym do his nycetee.
And therfore every man this tale I telle,
Wynne whoso may, for al is for to selle;
With empty hand men may none haukes lure.
For wynnyng wolde I al his lust endure,   416
And make me a feyned appetit;
And yet in bacon hadde I nevere delit.

402 **kyndely:** naturally
403 **avaunte me:** boast
404 **in ech degree:** in all respects
406 **murmur:** grumbling **grucchyng:** complaining
407 **abedde:** in bed
411 **maad his raunson:** paid his penalty
412 **nycetee:** foolishness, lust
416 **wynnyng:** profit
417 **feyned:** pretended
418 **bacon:** bacon (i.e., preserved old meat)

That made me that evere I wolde hem chide,
For thogh the pope hadde seten hem biside,
I wolde nat spare hem at hir owene bord,   421
For, by my trouthe, I quitte hem word for
      word.
As helpe me verray God omnipotent,
Though I right now sholde make my testament,
I ne owe hem nat a word that it nys quit.   425
I broghte it so aboute by my wit
That they moste yeve it up, as for the beste,
Or elles hadde we nevere been in reste;
For thogh he looked as a wood leon,
Yet sholde he faille of his conclusion.   430
    Thanne wolde I seye, 'Goode lief, taak keep
How mekely looketh Wilkyn, oure sheep!
Com neer, my spouse, lat me ba thy cheke!
Ye sholde been al pacient and meke,
And han a sweete spiced conscience,   435

---

421 **bord:** table
422 **quitte:** repaid
424 **testament:** will
430 **faille of his conclusion:** fail to attain his goal
431 **Goode lief:** sweetheart
432 **mekely:** meekly **Wilkyn:** Willie
433 **neer:** nearer **ba:** kiss
435 **spiced:** scrupulous

Sith ye so preche of Jobes patience.

Suffreth alwey, syn ye so welk an preche;

And but ye do, certein we shal yow teche

That it is fair to have a wyf in pees.

Oon of us two moste bowen, doutelees,   440

And sith a man is moore resonable

Than womman is, ye moste been suffrable.

What eyleth yow to grucche thus and grone?

Is it for ye wolde have my queynte allone?

Wy, taak it al! Lo, have it every deel!   445

Peter! I shrewe yow, but ye love it weel;

For if I wolde selle my *bele chose*,

I koude walke as fressh as is a rose;

But I wol kepe it for youre owene tooth.

Ye be to blame, by God! I sey yow sooth.'   450

    Swiche manere wordes hadde we on honde.

Now wol I speken of my fourthe housbonde.

    My fourthe housbonde was a revelour—

---

436 **Jobes:** (the biblical) Job's
442 **suffrable:** able to bear suffering
444 **queynte:** elegant, pleasing thing (sexual favors)
445 **have it every deel:** have every bit of it
446 **Peter!:** by, in the name of, St. Peter **shrewe yow, but ye:** curse you unless you (if you do not)
447 **bele chose:** beautiful thing (sexual favors)
449 **tooth:** taste, pleasure
450 **I sey yow sooth:** I am telling you the truth
453 **revelour:** reveller, profligate

This is to seyn, he hadde a paramour—
And I was yong and ful of ragerye,   455
Stibourn and strong, and joly as a pye.
How koude I daunce to an harpe smale,
And synge, ywis, as any nyghtyngale,
Whan I had dronke a draughte of sweete wyn!
Metellius, the foule cherl, the swyn,   460
That with a staf birafte his wyf hir lyf,
For she drank wyn, thogh I hadde been his wyf,
He sholde nat han daunted me fro drynke!
And after wyn on Venus moste I thynke,
For al so siker as cold engendreth hayl,   465
A likerous mouth moste han a likerous tayl.
In wommen vinolent is no defence—
This knowen lecchours by experience.
    But—Lord Crist!—whan that it remem-
        breth me

---

454 **paramour:** lady-love, concubine
455 **ragerye:** wantonness
456 **Stibourn:** stubborn   **pye:** magpie
460 **Metellius:** Egnatius Metellius   **cherl:** villain
461 **birafte:** took away from
462 **thogh:** although if
463 **daunted:** frightened
465 **al so siker as:** as surely as
466 **likerous mouth:** a gluttonous mouth   **likerous tayl:** lecherous tail
467 **vinolent:** drunken
469 **it remembreth me:** I remember

Upon my yowthe, and on my jolitee,   470
It tikleth me aboute myn herte roote.
Unto this day it dooth myn herte boote
That I have had my world as in my tyme.
But age, allas, that al wole envenyme,
Hath me biraft by beautee and my pith.   475
Lat go. Farewel! The devel go therwith!
The flour is goon; ther is namoore to telle;
The bren, as I best kan, now moste I selle;
But yet to be right myrie wol I fonde.
Now wol I tellen of my fourthe housbonde.

   I seye, I hadde in hene greet despit   481
That he of any oother had delit.
But he was quit, by God and by Seint Joce!
I made hym of the same wode a croce;
Nat of my body, in no foul manere,   485
But certeinly, I made folk swich cheere
That in his owene grece I made hym frye

471 **herte roote:** the bottom of my heart
472 **dooth myn herte boote:** does my heart good
474 **envenyme:** poison
475 **biraft:** taken away   **pith:** vigor
478 **bren:** bran
479 **fonde:** try
483 **Seint Joce:** St Judocus
484 **croce:** cross
487 **grece:** grease

For angre, and for verray jalousye.
By God, in erthe I was his purgatorie,
For which I hope his soule be in glorie.   490
For, God it woot, he sat ful ofte and song,
Whan that his shoo ful bitterly hym wrong.
Ther was no wight, save God and he, that
          wiste,
In many wise, how soore I hym twiste.
He deyde whan I cam fro Jerusalem,   495
And lith ygrave under the roode beem,
Al is his tombe noght so curyus
As was the sepulcre of hym Daryus,
Which that Appelles wroghte subtilly;
It nys but wast to burye hym preciously.   500
Lat hym fare wel; God yeve his soule reste!
He is now in his grave and in his cheste.
     Now of my fifthe housbonde wol I telle.

490 **hope:** suppose
492 **wrong:** pinched
493 **wiste:** knew
494 **twiste:** tortured
495 **deyde:** died
496 **ygrave:** buried   **roode beem:** beam supporting the cross at the entrance to the choir
     of the church
498 **sepulcre:** sepulcher   **hym Daryus:** that Darius
499 **Appelles:** the Jewish craftsman supposedly responsible for Darius's tomb
500 **preciously:** expensively
502 **cheste:** coffin

God lete his soule nevere come in helle!

And yet was he to me the mooste shrewe; 505

That feele I on my ribbes al by rewe,

And evere shal unto myn endyng day.

But in oure bed he was so fressh and gay,

And therwithal so wel koude he me glose,

Whan that he wolde han my *bele chose*, 510

That thogh he hadde me bete on every bon,

He koude wynne agayn my love anon.

I trowe I loved hym best, for that he

Was of his love daungerous to me.

We wommen han, if that I shal nat lye, 515

In this matere a queynte fantasye:

Wayte what thyng we may nat lightly have,

Therafter wol we crie al day and crave.

Forbede us thyng, and that desiren we;

Preesse on us faste, and thanne wol we fle. 520

With daunger oute we al oure chaffare;

---

505 **mooste shrewe:** greatest scoundrel
506 **by rewe:** in a row, one after another
509 **glose:** flatter
510 **bele chose:** beautiful thing (sexual favors)
514 **daungerous:** standoffish, hard to get
516 **queynte fantasye:** curious, strange inclination
517 **Wayte what:** note that whatever **lightly:** easily
520 **Preesse:** press, entreat
521 Grudgingly (*daunger*) we spread out (*oute*) all our merchandise (*chaffare*).

Greet prees at market maketh deere ware,
And to greet cheep is holde at litel prys:
This knoweth every womman that is wys.   524
    My fifthe housbonde—God his soule
        blesse!—
Which that I took for love, and no richesse,
He som tyme was a clerk of Oxenford,
And hadde left scole, and wente at horn to bord
With my gossib, dwellynge in oure toun;
God have hir soule! Hir name was Alisoun.   530
She knew myn herte, and eek my privetee,
Bet than oure parisshe preest, so moot I thee!
To hire biwreyed I my conseil al.
For hadde myn housbonde pissed on a wal,
Or doon a thyng that sholde han cost his lyf,
To hire, and to another worthy wyf,   536
And to my nece, which that I loved weel,
I wolde han toold his conseil every deel.
And so I dide ful often, God it woot,
That made his face often reed and hoot   540

522 **prees:** crowd   **deere:** expensive
523 **to greet cheep:** too good a bargain
527 **som tyme:** once, formerly
529 **gossib:** close friend
533 **biwreyed:** revealed

For verray shame, and blamed hymself for he
Had toold to me so greet a pryvetee.
    And so bifel that ones in a Lente—
So often tymes I to my gossyb wente,
For evere yet I loved to be gay,   545
And for to walke in March, Averill, and May,
Fro hous to hous, to heere sondry talys—
That Jankyn clerk, and my gossyb dame Alys,
And I myself, into the feeldes wente.
Myn housbonde was at Londoun al that Lente;
I hadde the bettre leyser for to pleye,   551
And for to se, and eek for to be seye
Of lusty folk. What wiste I wher my grace
Was shapen for to be, or in what place?
Therfore I made my visitaciouns   555
To vigilies and to processiouns,
To prechyng eek, and to thise pilgrimages,
To pleyes of myracles, and to mariages,
And wered upon my gaye scarlet gytes.   559

542 **pryvetee:** secret
551 **leyser:** leisure, opportunity
552 **seye:** seen
554 **shapen:** destined
556 **vigilies:** gatherings on the evenings before religious holidays
558 **pleyes of myracles:** popular dramas on religious subjects
559 **gytes:** robes

Thise wormes, ne thise motthes, ne thise mytes,
Upon my peril, frete hem never a deel;
And wostow why? For they were used weel.
  Now wol I tellen forth what happed me.
I seye that in the feeldes walked we,
Til trewely we hadde swich daliance,   565
This clerk and I, that of my purveiance
I spak to hym and seyde hym how that he,
If I were wydwe, sholde wedde me.
For certainly—I sey for no bobance—
Yet was I nevere withouten purveiance   570
Of mariage, n'of othere thynges eek.
I holde a mouses herte nat worth a leek
That hath but oon hole for to sterte to,
And if that faille, thanne is al ydo.   574
  I bar hym on honde he hadde enchanted
        me—
My dame taughte me that soutiltee—
And eek I seyde I mette of hym al nyght,
He wolde han slayn me as I lay upright,

---

560 **motthes:** moths **mytes:** small insects
561 **Upon my peril:** (I swear) on peril (of my soul) **frete:** devoured **never a deel:** not a bit
565 **daliance:** flirtation
566 **purveiance:** foresight, provision
569 **bobance:** boast
576 **dame:** mother **soutiltee:** subtlety, trick
577 **mette:** dreamed

And al my bed was ful of verray blood;
'But yet I hope that ye shal do me good,   580
For blood bitokeneth gold, as me was taught.'
And al was fals; I dremed of it right naught,
But as I folwed ay my dames loore,
As wel of this as of othere thynges moore.
    But now, sire, lat me se what I shal seyn.
A ha! By God, I have my tale ageyn.   586
    Whan that my fourthe housbonde was on
        beere,
I weep algate, and made sory cheere,
As wyves mooten, for it is usage,
And with my coverchief covered my visage,
But for that I was purveyed of a make,   591
I wepte but smal, and that I undertake.
    To chirche was myn housbonde born
        a-morwe
With neighebores, that for hym maden sorwe;
And Jankyn, oure clerk, was oon of tho.   595
As help me God, whan that I saugh hym go

582 **right naught:** not at all
587 **beere:** bier
588 **algate:** continuously
591 **purveyed of:** provided with beforehand
592 **smal:** little **undertake:** affirm, declare
593 **a-morwe:** next morning

After the beere, me thoughte he hadde a paire
Of legges and of feet so clene and faire
That al myn herte I yaf unto his hoold.
He was, I trowe, twenty wynter oold,   600
And I was fourty, if I shal seye sooth;
But yet I hadde alwey a coltes tooth.
Gat-tothed I was, and that bicam me weel;
I hadde the prente of seinte Venus seel.
As help me God, I was a lusty oon,   605
And faire, and riche, and yong, and wel bigon,
And trewely, as myne housbondes tolde me,
I hadde the beste *quoniam* myghte be.
For certes, I am al Venerien
In feelynge, and myn herte is Marcien.   610
Venus me yaf my lust, my likerousnesse,
And Mars yaf me my sturdy hardynesse;
Myn ascendent was Taur, and Mars therinne.

599 **hoold:** keeping
600 **wynter:** years
602 **coltes tooth:** youthful tastes, desires
603 **Gat-tothed:** with teeth set wide apart
604 **prente:** imprint, mark   **Venus seel:** Venus's mark, a birthmark
606 **wel bigon:** in a good situation
608 **quoniam:** whatsit (literally, *because* or *whereas*), a euphemism
609 **Venerien:** dominated by the planet Venus
610 **Marcien:** dominated by the planet Mars
612 **hardynesse:** boldness
613 **ascendent was Taur:** ascending sign was Taurus, the bull

Allas, allas! That evere love was synne!
I folwed ay myn inclinacioun   615
By vertu of my constellacioun;
That made me I koude noght withdrawe
My chambre of Venus from a good felawe.
Yet have I Martes mark upon my face,
And also in another privee place.   620
For God so wys be my savacioun,
I ne loved nevere by no discrecioun,
But evere folwede myn appetit,
Al were he short, or long, or blak, or whit;
I took no kep, so that he liked me,   625
How poore he was, ne eek of what degree.
    What sholde I seye but, at the months
          ende,
This joly clerk, Jankyn, that was so hende,
Hath wedded me with greet solempnytee,
And to hym yaf I al the lond and fee   630

615 **inclinacioun:** astrologically determined inclination
616 **constellacioun:** configuration of the heavenly bodies, horoscope
617 **withdrawe:** withhold
619 **Martes mark:** mark of Mars, a reddish birthmark
620 **privee:** secret
621 **God so wys be:** as may God surely be   **savacioun:** salvation
622 **discrecioun:** moderation, prudence
625 **so that:** providing that
628 **hende:** courteous
630 **fee:** property

That evere was me yeven therbifoore.
But afterward repented me ful soore;
He nolde suffre nothyng of my list.
By God, he smoot me ones on the lyst,
For that I rente out of his book a leef,   635
That of the strook myn ere wax al deef.
Stibourn I was as is a leonesse,
And of my tonge a verray jangleresse,
And walke I wolde, as I had doon biforn,   639
From hous to hous, although he had it sworn;
For which he often tymes wolde preche,
And me of olde Romayn geestes teche;
How he Symplicius Gallus lefte his wyf,
And hire forsook for terme of al his lyf,
Noght but for open-heveded he hir say   645
Lookynge out at his dore upon a day.

Another Romayn tolde he me by name,

633 **list:** desires
634 **lyst:** ear
635 **rente:** tore
637 **Stibourn:** stubborn
638 **jangleresse:** chatterbox
640 **it sworn:** sworn the contrary
642 **geestes:** stories
643 **Symplicius Gallus:** His story is told by Valerius Maximus, as is the incident in 647
    below.
645 **open-heveded:** bareheaded **say:** saw
647 **Another Romayn:** See 643 above.

That, for his wyf was at a someres game
Withouten his wityng, he forsook hire eke.
And thanne wolde he upon his Bible seke   650
That ilke proverbe of Ecclesiaste
Where he comandeth and forbedeth faste
Man shal nat suffre his wyf go roule aboute.
Thanne wolde he seye right thus, withouten
      doute:
  'Whoso that buyldeth his hous al of salwes,
And priketh his blynde hors over the falwes,
And suffreth his wyf to go seken halwes,   657
Is worthy to been hanged on the galwes!'
But al for noght, I sette noght an hawe
Of his proverbes n'of his olde sawe,   660
Ne I wolde nat of hym corrected be.
I hate hym that my vices telleth me,
And so doo mo, God woot, of us than I.

648 **someres game:** midsummer revels
649 **wityng:** knowledge
651 **Ecclesiaste:** Ecclesiasticus
652 **he:** the author of Ecclesiasticus
653 **roule:** wander
655 **salwes:** willow branches
656 **falwes:** open fields (idle land)
657 **seken halwes:** go on pilgrimages
659 **hawe:** haw, hawthorn berry (i.e., nothing)

This made hym with me wood al outrely;
I nolde noght forbere hym in no cas.   665

   Now wol I seye yow sooth, by Seint Thomas,
Why that I rente out of his book a leef,
For which he smoot me so that I was deef.

   He hadde a book that gladly, nyght and day,
For his desport he wolde rede alway;   670
He cleped it Valerie and Theofraste,
At which book he lough alwey ful faste.
And eek ther was somtyme a clerk at Rome,
A cardinal, that highte Seint Jerome,
That made a book agayn Jovinian;   675
In which book eek ther was Tertulan,
Crisippus, Trotula, and Helowys,
That was abbesse nat fer fro Parys,
And eek the Parables of Salomon,

664 **al outrely:** entirely
665 **forbere:** put up with
671-80 **Valerie and Theofraste:** Valerius, supposed author of the *Dissuasio* (or *Epistola*) *ad Rufinum*, and Theophrastus, author of the *Golden Book on Marriage*, both works attacking marriage. Jankyn's book of "wicked wives" also contains passages from the book by *Jerome* (a father of the Church) *agayn Jovinian* (an unorthodox monk who denied that virginity was necessarily superior to marriage), *Tertulan* (Tertullian, whose works contain misogynist and anti-marriage passages), *Crisippus* (mentioned by Jerome but otherwise unknown), *Trotula* (probably Trotula di Ruggiero, a female physician and author), *Helou'ys* (Heloïse, lover of Abelard), *the Parables of Salomon* (Prov. 10.1 to 22.16 in the Vulgate), and *Ovides Art* (Ovid's *Ars amatoria*).
673 **clerk:** scholar

149

Ovides Art, and bookes many on,   680
And alle thise were bounden in o volume.
And every nyght and day was his custume,
Whan he hadde leyser and vacacioun
From oother worldly occupacioun,
To reden on this book of wikked wyves.   685
He knew of hem mo legendes and lyves
Than been of goode wyves in the Bible.
For trusteth wel, it is an impossible
That any clerk wol speke good of wyves,
But if it be of hooly seintes lyves,   690
Ne of noon oother womman never the mo.
Who peyntede the leon, tel me who?
By God, if wommen hadde writen stories,
As clerkes han withinne hire oratories,
They wolde han writen of men moore wikked-
          nesse
Than al the mark of Adam may redresse.   696

683 **vacacioun:** spare time
688 **impossible:** impossibility
689 **clerk:** learned man, clergyman
691 **never the mo:** in any way
692 The lion's question when he saw a picture of a man killing a lion
693 **stories:** histories
694 **oratories:** chapels
696 **mark of Adam:** male sex

The children of Mercurie and of Venus
Been in hir wirkyng ful contrarius;
Mercurie loveth wysdam and science,
And Venus loveth ryot and dispence. 700
And, for hire diverse disposicioun,
Ech falleth in otheres exaltacioun.
And thus, God woot, Mercurie is desolat
In Pisces, wher Venus is exaltat,
And Venus falleth ther Mercurie is reysed. 705
Therfore no womman of no clerk is preysed.
The clerk, whan he is oold, and may noght do
Of Venus werkes worth his olde sho,
Thanne sit he doun, and writ in his dotage
That wommen kan nat kepe hir mariage! 710
      But now to purpos, why I tolde thee
That I was beten for a book, pardee!
Upon a nyght Jankyn, that was oure sire,

697 **children of Mercurie:** those dominated by the planet Mercury (scholars)   **of Venus:** those dominated by Venus, lovers
698 **wirkyng ful contrarius:** actions directly contrary
699 **science:** knowledge
700 **ryot:** debauchery   **dispence:** extravagant expenditures
702 **exaltacioun:** the zodiacal sign in which a planet is most powerful
703 **desolat:** powerless
704 **Pisces:** the zodiacal sign   **exaltat:** exalted (has her exaltation, is most powerful)
711 **now to purpos:** now to the point
713 **oure sire:** master of our house

Redde on his book, as he sat by the fire,
Of Eva first, that for hir wikkednesse   715
Was al mankynde broght to wrecchednesse,
For which that Jhesu Crist hymself was slayn,
That boghte us with his herte blood agayn.
Lo, heere expres of womman may ye fynde
That womman was the los of al mankynde.   720
    Tho redde he me how Sampson loste his
      heres:
Slepynge, his lemman kitte it with hir sheres;
Thurgh which treson loste he bothe his yen.
    Tho redde he me, if that I shal nat lyen,
Of Hercules and of his Dianyre,   725
That caused hym to sette hymself afyre.
    No thyng forgat he the care and the wo
That Socrates hadde with his wyves two,
How Xantippa caste pisse upon his heed.
This sely man sat Stille as he were deed;   730
He wiped his heed, namoore dorste he seyn,

---

715 **Eva:** Eve
719 **expres:** clearly
721 **Sampson:** For the story see "The Monk's Tale" in *The Canterbury Tales*.
725 **Hercules and . . . Dianyre:** For the story see "The Monk's Tale" in *The Canterbury Tales*.
729 **Xantippa:** Xantippe, shrewish wife of Socrates, the Greek philosopher

But 'Er that thonder stynte, comth a reyn!'

    Of Phasipha, that was the queene of Crete,

For shrewednesse, hym thoughte the tale

        swete;

Fy! Spek namoore—it is a grisly thyng—   735

Of hire horrible lust and hir likyng.

    Of Clitermystra, for hire lecherye,

That falsly made hire housbonde for to dye,

He redde it with ful good devocioun.

    He tolde me eek for what occasioun   740

Amphiorax at Thebes loste his lyf.

Myn housbonde hadde a legende of his wyf,

Eriphilem, that for an ouche of gold

Hath prively unto the Grekes told

Wher that hir housbonde hidde hym in a place,

For which he hadde at Thebes sory grace.   746

    Of Lyvia tolde he me, and of Lucye:

They bothe made hir housbondes for to dye,

---

733 **Phasipha:** Pasiphae, mother of the Minotaur, fathered on her by a bull

734 **shrewednesse:** malignancy

737 **Clitermystra:** Clytemnestra murdered her husband Agamemnon, the Greek king who waged war against Troy.

741 **Amphiorax:** Amphiaraus died at Thebes because he took the advice of his wife, Eriphyle (*Eriphilem*).

743 **ouche:** brooch

746 **sory grace:** misfortune

747 **Lyvia:** Livia, lover of Sejanus   **Lucye:** Lucia, wife of the Roman poet Lucretius

That oon for love, that oother was for hate.
Lyvia hir housbonde, on an even late,   750
Empoysoned hath, for that she was his fo;
Lucia, likerous, loved hire housbonde so
That, for he sholde alwey upon hire thynke,
She yaf hym swich a manere love-drynke
That he was deed er it were by the morwe;
And thus algates housbondes han sorwe.   756

   Thanne tolde he me how oon Latumyus
Compleyned unto his felawe Arrius
That in his gardyn growed swich a tree
On which he seyde how that his wyves thre
Hanged hemself for herte despitus.   761
'O leeve brother,' quod this Arrius,
'Yif me a plante of thilke blissed tree,
And in my gardyn planted shal it bee.'

   Of latter date, of wyves hath he red.   765
That somme han slayn hir housbondes in hir
          bed,
And lete hir lecchour dighte hire al the nyght,
Whan that the corps lay in the floor upright.
And somme han dryve nayles in hir brayn,

---

751 **Empoysoned:** poisoned
756 **algates:** always
767 **dighte:** copulate with

Whil that they slepte, and thus they had hem
     slayn.   770
Somme han hem yeve poysoun in hire drynke.
He spak moore harm than herte may bithynke,
And therwithal he knew of mo proverbs
Than in this world ther growen gras or herbes.
'Bet is,' quod he, 'thyn habitacioun   775
Be with a leon or a foul dragoun,
Than with a womman usynge for to chyde.
Bet is,' quod he, 'hye in the roof abyde,
Than with an angry wyf doun in the hous;
They been so wikked and contrarious,   780
They haten that hir housbondes loven ay.'
He seyde, 'A womman cast hir shame away,
Whan she cast of hir smok'; and forthermo,
'A fair womman, but she be chaast also,
Is lyk a gold ryng in a sowes nose.'   785
Who wolde wene, or who wolde suppose,
The wo that in myn herte was, and pyne?
   And whan I saugh he wolde nevere fyne
To reden on this cursed book al nyght,

772 **harm:** slander   **bithynke:** imagine
777 **usynge for to:** used to
783 **smok:** shift, undergarment
788 **fyne:** cease

Al sodeynly thre leves have I plyght 790
Out of his book, right as he radde, and eke
I with my fest so took hym on the cheke
That in oure fyr he fil bakward adoun.
And he up stirte as dooth a wood leoun,
And with his fest he smoot me on the heed
That in the floor I lay as I were deed. 796
And whan he saugh how stille that I lay,
He was agast and wolde han fled his way,
Til atte laste out of my swogh I breyde.
'O! hastow slayn me, false theef?' I seyde, 800
'And for my land thus hastow mordred me?
Er I be deed, yet wol I kisse thee.'

    And neer he cam, and kneled faire adoun,
And seyde, 'Deere suster Alisoun,
As help me God, I shal thee nevere smyte!
That I have doon, it is thyself to wyte. 806
Foryeve it me, and that I thee biseke!'
And yet eftsoones I hitte hym on the cheke,
And seyde, 'Theef, thus muchel am I wreke;

790 **plyght:** plucked
791 **radde:** read
792 **took hym:** gave him (a blow)
799 **swogh:** swoon   **breyde:** started up, awoke
806 **to wyte:** to blame
808 **eftsoones:** immediately
809 **wreke:** avenged

Now wol I dye, I may no lenger speke.'   810
But atte laste, with muchel care and wo,
We fille acorded by us selven two.
He yaf me al the bridel in myn hond,
To han the governance of hous and lond,
And of his tonge, and of his hond also;   815
And made hym brenne his book anon right tho.
And whan that I hadde geten unto me,
By maistrie, al the soveraynetee,
And that he seyde, 'Myn owene trewe wyf,
Do as thee lust the terme of al thy lyf;   820
Keep thyn honour, and keep eek myn estaat'—
After that day we hadden never debaat.
God helpe me so, I was to hym as kynde
As any wyf from Denmark unto Ynde,
And also trewe, and so was he to me.   825
I prey to God, that sit in magestee,
So blesse his soule for his mercy deere.
Now wol I seye my tale, if ye wol heere."

Biholde the wordes bitwene the
Somonour and the Frere.

The Frere lough, whan he hadde herd al this;
"Now dame," quod he, "so have I joye or blis,

---

818 **soveraynetee:** sovereignty, mastery
824 **Denmark unto Ynde:** throughout the whole world

This is a long preamble of a tale!"   831
And whan the Somonour herde the Frere gale,
"Lo," quod the Somonour, "Goddes armes two!
A frere wol entremette hym everemo.
Lo, goode men, a flye and eek a frere   835
Wol falle in every dyssh and eek mateere.
What spekestow of preambulacioun?
What! amble, or trotte, or pees, or go sit doun!
Thou lettest oure disport in this manere."
    "Ye, woltow so, sire Somonour?" quod the
              Frere;
"Now, by my feith I shal, er that I go,   841
Telle of a somonour swich a tale or two
That alle the folk shal laughen in this place."
    "Now elles, Frere, I bishrewe thy face,"
Quod this Somonour, "and I bishrewe me,   845
But if I telle tales two or thre
Of freres er I come to Sidyngborne

832 **gale:** cry out
834 **entremette hym:** interfere
837 **preambulacioun:** making a preamble
838 **amble, or trotte, or pees:** amble (an easy lateral walk on horseback; i.e., go slow),
    trot (i.e., go fast), or keep still
839 **lettest:** hinder
844 **bishrewe:** curse
847 **Sidyngborne:** Sittingbourne, a town between Rochester and Canterbury, about 40
    miles from London

That I shal make thyn herte for to morne,
For wel I woot thy pacience is gon."   849

    Oure Hooste cride "Pees! And that anon!"
And seyde, "Lat the womman telle hire tale.
Ye fare as folk that dronken ben of ale.
Do, dame, telle forth youre tale, and that is
      best."

    "Al redy, sire," quod she, right as yow lest,
If I have licence of this worthy Frere."   855

    "Yis, dame," quod he, "tel forth, and I wol
      heere."

Heere endeth the Wyf of Bathe hir Prologe.

848 **morne:** mourn
852 **fare:** act
856 **Yis:** yes indeed

The Wife of Bath's Tale

HEERE BIGYNNETH THE TALE OF THE WYF OF BATHE.

In th'olde dayes of the Kyng Arthour,
Of which that Britons speken greet honour,
Al was this land fulfild of fayerye.
The elf-queene, with hir joly compaignye,   860
Daunced ful ofte in many a grene mede.
This was the olde opinion, as I rede;
I speke of manye hundred yeres ago.
But now kan no manse none elves mo,
For now the grete charitee and prayeres   865
Of lymytours and othere hooly freres,
That serchen every lond and every streem,
As thikke as motes in the sonne-beem,
Blessynge halles, chambres, kichenes, boures,

859 The whole country was filled with fairies.
860 **elf-queene:** fairy queen
866 **lymytours:** friars
867 **serchen:** haunt
868 **motes:** specks of dust
869 **boures:** bedrooms

Citees, burghes, castels, hye toures,   870
Thropes, bernes, shipnes, dayeryes—
This maketh that ther ben no fayeryes.
For ther as wont to walken was an elf
Ther walketh now the lymytour hymself
In undermeles and in morwenynges,   875
And seyth his matyns and his hooly thynges
As he gooth in his lymytacioun.
Wommen may go saufly up and doun.
In every bussh or under every tree
Ther is noon oother incubus but he,   880
And he ne wol doon hem but dishonour.
        And so bifel that this kyng Arthour
Hadde in his hous a lusty bacheler,
That on a day cam ridynge fro ryver,
And happed that, allone as he was born,   885
He saugh a mayde walkynge hym biforn,
Of which mayde anon, maugree hir heed,

870 **burghes:** boroughs
871 **Thropes:** villages **bernes:** barns **shipnes:** stables **dayeryes:** dairies
875 **undermeles:** late mornings (from 9 to 12) **morwenynges:** mornings
876 **matyns:** matins, morning prayers
877 **lymytacioun:** territory
878 **saufly:** safely
880 **incubus:** evil spirit, said to copulate with women
883 **bacheler:** young knight
884 **ryver:** hawking for waterfowl
887 **maugree hir heed:** against her will, despite all she could do

By verray force, he rafte hire maydenhed;
For which oppressioun was swich clamour
And swich pursute unto the kyng Arthour   890
That dampned was this knyght for to be deed,
By cours of lawe, and sholde han lost his
         heed—
Paraventure swich was the statut tho—
But that the queene and other ladyes mo
So longe preyeden the kyng of grace   895
Til he his lyf hym graunted in the place,
And yaf hym to the queene, al at hir wille,
To chese wheither she wolde hym save or
         spille.
   The queene thanketh the kyng with al hir
         myght,
And after this thus spak she to the knyght,   900
Whan that she saugh hir tyme, upon a day:
"Thou standest yet," quod she, "in swich array
That of thy lyf yet hastow no suretee.
I grante thee lyf, if thou kanst tellen me   904

888 **rafte:** took
889 **oppressioun:** wrong
890 **pursute:** suing for justice

893 **Paraventure:** perhaps
898 **spille:** put to death
903 **suretee:** security

What thyng is it that wommen moost desiren.
Be war, and keep thy nekke-boon from iren!
And if thou kanst nat tellen it anon,
Yet wol I yeve thee leve for to gon
A twelf-month and a day, to seche and leere
An answere suffisant in this mateere;   910
And suretee wol I han, er that thou pace,
Thy body for to yelden in this place."

   Wo was this knyght, and sorwefully he siketh;
But what! He may nat do al as hym liketh.
And at the laste he chees hym for to wende
And come agayn, right at the yeres ende,   916
With swich answere as God wolde hym pur-
       veye;
And taketh his leve, and wendeth forth his
       weye.

   He seketh every hous and every place
Where as he hopeth for to fynde grace   920
To lerne what thyng wommen loven moost,
But he ne koude arryven in no coost

---

906 **iren:** iron (i.e., the executioner's axe)
909 **seche:** search **leere:** learn
911 **suretee:** pledge
912 **yelden:** surrender
917 **purveye:** provide
922 **coost:** coast (region)

Wher as he myghte fynde in this mateere
Two creatures accordynge in-feere.   924
Somme seyde wommen loven best richesse,
Somme seyde honour, somme seyde jolynesse,
Somme riche array, somme seyden lust abedde,
And oftetyme to be wydwe and wedde.
Somme seyde that oure hertes been moost esed
Whan that we been yflatered and yplesed.   930
He gooth ful ny the sothe, I wol nat lye.
A man shal wynne us best with flaterye,
And with attendance and with bisynesse
Been we ylymed, bothe moore and lesse.

   And somme seyen that we loven best   935
For to be free and do right as us lest,
And that no man repreve us of oure vice,
But seye that we be wise and no thyng nyce.
For trewely ther is noon of us alle,
If any wight wol clawe us on the galle,   940
That we nel kike, for he seith us sooth.

---

924 **accordynge in-feere:** agreeing together, in agreement
931 **gooth ful ny the sothe:** gets very close to the truth
933 **attendance:** attention
934 **ylymed:** caught (as with bird-lime)
936 **us lest:** we please
937 **repreve:** reprove
940 **clawe us on the galle:** rub a sore spot
941 **nel kike:** will not (*nel = ne u il*) kick back

Assay, and he shal fynde it that so dooth;
For, be we never so vicious withinne,
We wol been holden wise and clene of synne.

And somme seyn that greet delit han we   945
For to been holden stable, and eek secree,
And in o purpos stedefastly to dwelle,
And nat biwreye thyng that men us telle.
But that tale is nat worth a rake-stele.
Pardee, we wommen konne no thyng hele;   950
Witnesse on Myda—wol ye heere the tale?

Ovyde, amonges othere thynges smale,
Seyde Myda hadde, under his longe heres,
Growynge upon his heed two asses eres,   954
The whiche vice he hydde as he best myghte
Ful subtilly from every mannes sighte,
That, save his wyf, ther wiste of it namo.
He loved hire moost, and trusted hire also;
He preyede hire that to no creature
She sholde tellen of his disfigure.   960

---

944 **holden:** considered
946 **secree:** discreet, able to keep a secret
948 **biwreye:** betray, reveal
949 **rake-stele:** rake handle (i.e., nothing)
950 **hele:** keep secret
951 **Witnesse on:** take the evidence of   **Myda:** Midas
952 **Ovyde:** Ovid, the Roman poet
960 **disfigure:** deformity

She swoor him, "Nay"; for al this world to
  wynne,
She nolde do that vileynye or synne,
To make hir housbonde han so foul a name.
She nolde nat telle it for hir owene shame.
But nathelees, hir thoughte that she dyde   965
That she so longe sholde a conseil hyde;
Hir thoughte it swal so soore aboute hir herte
That nedely som word hire moste asterte;
And sith she dorste telle it to no man,
Doun to a mareys faste by she ran—   970
Til she cam there hir herte was afyre—
And as a bitore bombleth in the myre,
She leyde hir mouth unto the water doun:
"Biwreye me nat, thou water, with thy soun,"
Quod she; "to thee I telle it and namo;   975
Myn housbonde hath longe asses erys two!
Now is myn herte al hool; now is it oute.
I myghte no lenger kepe it, out of doute."

965 **dyde:** would die
966 **conseil:** secret
967 **swal:** swelled
968 **nedely:** of necessity **asterte:** escape
970 **mareys:** marsh
972 **bitore bombleth in the myre:** bittern bumbles (booms) in the mire
974 **Biwreye:** betray **soun:** sound

Heere may ye se, thogh we a tyme abyde,
Yet out it moot; we kan no conseil hyde.   980
The remenant of the tale if ye wol heere,
Redeth Ovyde, and ther ye may it leere.

   This knyght, of which my tale is specially,
Whan that he saugh he myghte nat come
       therby—
This is to seye, what wommen love moost—   985
Withinne his brest ful sorweful was the goost.
But hoom he gooth; he myghte nat sojourne;
The day was come that homward moste he
       tourne.
And in his wey it happed hym to ryde,
In al this care, under a forest syde,   990
Wher as he saugh upon a daunce go
Of ladyes foure and twenty, and yet mo;
Toward the whiche daunce he drow ful yerne,
In hope that som wysdom sholde he lerne.
But certeinly, er he cam fully there,   995
Vanysshed was this daunce, he nyste where.
No creature saugh he that bar lyf,

982 **leere:** learn
987 **sojourne:** remain
989 **it happed hym:** he chanced
990 **under:** by, near
993 **yerne:** eagerly

Save on the grene he saugh sittynge a wyf—
A fouler wight ther may no man devyse.
Agayn the knyght this olde wyf gan ryse,   1000
And seyde, "Sire knyght, heer forth ne lith no
    wey.
Tel me what that ye seken, by youre fey!
Paraventure it may the bettre be;
Thise olde folk kan muchel thyng," quod she.
   "My leeve mooder," quod this knyght, "cer-
    teyn
I nam but deed but if that I kan seyn   1006
What thyng it is that wommen moost desire.
Koude ye me wisse, I wolde wel quite youre
    hire."
   "Plight me thy trouthe heere in myn hand,"
    quod she,
"The nexte thyng that I requere thee,   1010
Thou shalt it do, if it lye in thy myght,
And I wol telle it yow er it be nyght."

998 **wyf:** woman
999 **devyse:** imagine
1000 **Agayn:** toward (to meet)
1008 **wisse:** inform, instruct   **quite youre hire:** reward your efforts
1009 **Plight:** pledge
1010 **requere:** ask

"Have heer my trouthe," quod the knyght,
    "I grante."
"Thanne," quod she, "I dar me wel avante
Thy lyf is sauf, for I wol stonde therby;   1015
Upon my lyf, the queene wol seye as I.
Lat se which is the proudeste of hem alle
That wereth on a coverchief or a calle
That dar seye nay of that I shal thee teche.
Lat us go forth withouten lenger speche."
Tho rowned she a pistel in his ere,   1021
And bad hym to be glad and have no fere.
    Whan they be comen to the court, this
        knyght
Seyde he had holde his day, as he hadde hight,
And redy was his answere, as he sayde.   1025
Ful many a noble wyf, and many a mayde,
And many a wydwe, for that they been wise,
The queene hirself sittynge as a justise,
Assembled been, his answere for to heere;

1013 **grante:** consent
1014 **avante:** boast
1015 **sauf:** safe
1016 **seye as I:** say as I do, agree with me
1018 **calle:** hairnet worn as a headdress
1021 **rowned:** whispered **pistel:** message
1024 **hight:** promised

And afterward this knyght was bode appeere.
   To every wight comanded was silence,   1031
And that the knyght sholde telle in audience
What thyng that worldly wommen loven best.
This knyght ne stood nat stille as doth a best,
But to his questioun anon answerde   1035
With manly voys, that al the court it herde:
   "My lige lady, generally," quod he,
"Wommen desiren to have sovereynetee
As wel over hir housbond as hir love,
And for to been in maistrie hym above.   1040
This is youre mooste desir, thogh ye me kille.
Dooth as yow list; I am heer at youre wille."
In al the court ne was ther wyf, ne mayde,
Ne wydwe that contraried that he sayde,
But seyden he was worthy han his lyf.   1045
And with that word up stirte the olde wyf,
Which that the knyght saugh sittynge on the
        grene:
"Mercy," quod she, "my sovereyn lady queene!
Er that youre court departe, do me right.
I taughte this answere unto the knyght;   1050

1030 **bode appeere:** commanded to appear
1034 **best:** beast
1044 **contraried:** denied

For which he plighte me his trouthe there,
The firste thyng that I wolde hym requere
He wolde it do, if it lay in his myghte.
Bifore the court thanne preye I thee, sir
      knyght,"
Quod she, "that thou me take unto thy wyf,
For wel thou woost that I have kept thy lyf.
If I seye fals, sey nay, upon thy fey!"   1057
   This knyght answerde, "Allas and weyla-
      wey!
I woot right wel that swich was my biheste.
For Goddes love, as chees a newe requeste!
Taak al my good and lat my body go."   1061
   "Nay, thanne," quod she, "I shrewe us bothe
      two!
For thogh that I be foul, and oold, and poore
I nolde for al the metal, ne for oore
That under erthe is grave or lith above,   1065
But if thy wyf I were, and eek thy love."
   "My love?" quod he, "nay, my dampna-
      cioun!

1051 **plighte:** pledged
1059 **biheste:** promise
1060 **as chees:** choose
1064 **oore:** ore

Allas, that any of my nacioun
Sholde evere so foule disparaged be!"
But al for noght; the ende is this, that he   1070
Constreyned was; he nedes moste hire wedde,
And taketh his olde wyf, and gooth to bedde.

    Now wolden som men seye, paraventure,
That for my necligence I do no cure
To tellen yow the joye and al th' array   1075
That at the feeste was that ilke day.
To which thyng shortly answeren I shal:
I seye ther nas no joye ne feeste at al;
Ther nas but hevynesse and muche sorwe.
For prively he wedded hire on morwe,
And al day after hidde hym as an owle,   1081
So wo was hym, his wyf looked so foule.

    Greet was the wo the knyght hadde in his
        thoght,
Whan he was with his wyf abedde ybroght;
He walweth and he turneth to and fro.   1085
His olde wyf lay smylynge everemo,
And seyde, "O deere housbonde, benedicitee!
Fareth every knyght thus with his wyf as ye?
Is this the lawe of kyng Arthures hous?

1068 **nacioun:** family
1069 **disparaged:** degraded by a union with
    someone of lower birth

1075 **array:** rich display
1085 **walweth:** writhes

Is every knyght of his so dangerous?   1090
I am youre owene love and youre wyf;
I am she which that saved hath youre lyf,
And, certes, yet ne dide I yow nevere unright;
Why fare ye thus with me this firste nyght?
Ye faren lyk a man had lost his wit.   1095
What is my gilt? For Goddes love, tel it,
And it shal been amended, if I may."
   "Amended?" quod this knyght, "Allas, nay,
      nay!
It wol nat been amended nevere mo.
Thou art so loothly, and so oold also,   1100
And therto comen of so lough a kynde,
That litel wonder is thogh I walwe and wynde.
So wolde God myn herte wolde breste!"
   "Is this," quod she, "the cause of youre un-
      reste?"
   "Ye, certeinly," quod he, "no wonder is."
   "Now, sire," quod she, "I koude amende al
      this,   1106

1096 **gilt:** offense
1100 **loothly:** loathsome
1101 **comen of so lough a kynde:** descended from such base-born lineage
1102 **wynde:** twist about
1104 **unreste:** distress

If that me liste, er it were dayes thre,
So wel ye myghte bere yow unto me.
   "But, for ye speken of swich gentilesse
As is descended out of old richesse,   1110
That therfore sholden ye be gentil men,
Swich arrogance is nat worth an hen.
Looke who that is moost vertuous alway,
Pryvee and apert, and moost entendeth ay
To do the gentil dedes that he kan;   1115
Taak hym for the grettest gentil man.
Crist wole we clayme of hym oure gentillesse,
Nat of oure eldres for hire old richesse.
For thogh they yeve us al hir heritage,   1119
For which we clayme to been of heigh parage,
Yet may they nat biquethe for no thyng
To noon of us hir vertuous lyvyng,
That made hem gentil men ycalled be,
And bad us folwen hem in swich degree.
   "Wel kan the wise poete of Florence,   1125
That highte Dant, speken in this sentence.

1108 **so:** so that   **bere yow unto me:** behave towards me
1109 **gentillesse:** nobility
1114 **Pryvee and apert:** in private and public, in all circumstances   **entendeth:** strives
1120 **heigh parage:** noble lineage
1126 **Dant:** Dante Alighieri

Lo, in swich maner rym is Dantes tale:
'Ful selde up riseth by his branches smale
Prowesse of man, for God, of his goodnesse,
Wole that of hym we clayme oure gentil-
      lesse';   1130
For of oure eldres may we no thyng clayme
But temporel thyng, that man may hurte and
      mayme.
  "Eek every wight woot this as wel as I,
If gentillesse were planted narureelly
Unto a certeyn lynage doun the lyne,   1135
Pryvee and apert thanne wolde they nevere
      fyne
To doon of gentillesse the faire office;
They myghte do no vileynye or vice.
  "Taak fyr and ber it in the derkeste hous
Bitwix this and the mount of Kaukasous,   1140
And lat men shette the dores and go thenne;
Yet wole the fyr as faire lye and brenne
As twenty thousand men myghte it biholde;

1130 **Wole:** desires
1132 **mayme:** injure
1136 **fyne:** cease
1137 **office:** duties
1140 **Kaukasous:** the Caucasus mountains
1141 **thenne:** thence
1142 **lye:** blaze

His office natureel ay wol it holde,
Up peril of my lyf, til that it dye.   1145
   "Heere may ye se wel how that genterye
Is nat annexed to possessioun,
Sith folk ne doon hir operacioun
Alwey, as dooth the fyr, lo, in his kynde.   1149
For, God it woot, men may wel often fynde
A lordes sone do shame and vileynye;
And he that wole han pris of his gentrye,
For he was boren of a gentil hous
And hadde his eldres noble and vertuous,
And nel hymselven do no gentil dedis   1155
Ne folwen his gentil auncestre that deed is,
He nys nat gentil, be he due or erl,
For vileyns synful dedes make a cherl.
For gentillesse nys but renomee   1159
Of thyne auncestres, for hire heigh bountee,
Which is a strange thyng to thy persone.
Thy gentillesse cometh fro God allone.

1146 **genterye:** gentility
1147 **annexed to:** joined with
1148 **ne doon hir operacioun:** do not behave as they should
1152 **pris of his gentrye:** praise for his noble birth
1155 **nel** = *ne wyl*, will not
1159 **renomee:** renown
1160 **bountee:** goodness
1161 **strange thyng:** a thing foreign to, not naturally part of

Thanne comth oure verray gentillesse of grace;
It was no thyng biquethe us with oure place.
   "Thenketh hou noble, as seith Valerius, 1165
Was thilke Tullius Hostillius,
That out of poverte roos to heigh noblesse.
Reedeth Senek, and redeth eek Boece;
Ther shul ye seen expres that it no drede is
That he is gentil that dooth gentil dedis. 1170
And therfore, leeve housbonde, I thus con-
      clude:
Al were it that myne auncestres were rude,
Yet may the hye God, and so hope I,
Grante me grace to lyven vertuously.
Thanne am I gentil, whan that I bigynne 1175
To lyven vertuously and weyve synne.
   "And ther as ye of poverte me repreeve,
The hye God, on whom that we bileeve,
In wilful poverte chees to lyve his lyf.
And certes every man, mayden, or wyf 1180
May understonde that Jhesus, hevene kyng,

1165 **Valerius:** Valerius Maximus, the Roman author
1166 **Tullius Hostillius:** legendary third king of Rome
1168 **Senek:** Seneca, Roman author   **Boece:** Boethius
1172 **Al were:** even though   **rude:** humble
1176 **weyve:** abandon
1179 **wilful:** willing, voluntary

Ne wolde nat chese a vicious lyvyng.
Glad poverte is an honest thyng, certeyn;
This wole Senec and othere clerkes seyn.
Whoso that halt hym payd of his poverte,   1185
I holde hym riche, al hadde he nat a sherte.
He that coveiteth is a povre wight,
For he wolde han that is nat in his myght;
But he that noght hath, ne coveiteth have,
Is riche, although ye holde hym but a knave.
Verray poverte, it syngeth proprely;   1191
Juvenal seith of poverte myrily:
'The povre man, whan he goth by the weye,
Bifore the theves he may synge and pleye.'
Poverte is hateful good and, as I gesse,   1195
A ful greet bryngere out of bisynesse;
A greet amendere eek of sapience
To hym that taketh it in pacience.
Poverte is this, although it seme alenge:
Possessioun that no wight wol chalenge.   1200

1185 **halt hym payd:** is satisfied
1189 **have:** to have (anything)
1190 **knave:** peasant
1192 **Juvenal:** the Roman poet
1196 **bryngere out of bisynesse:** one that brings out, encourages, industry
1197 **amendere:** improver   **sapience:** wisdom
1199 **alenge:** miserable
1200 **chalenge:** claim

Poverte ful ofte, whan a man is lowe,
Maketh his God and eek hymself to knowe.
Poverte a spectacle is, as thynketh me,
Thurgh which he may his verray freendes see.
And therfore, sire, syn that I noght yow greve,
Of my poverte namoore ye me repreve.   1206

   "Now, sire, of elde ye repreve me;
And certes, sire, thogh noon auctoritee
Were in no book, ye gentils of honour
Seyn that men sholde an oold wight doon
      favour   1210
And clepe hym fader, for youre gentillesse;
And auctours shal I fynden, as I gesse.

   "Now ther ye seye that I am foul and old,
Than drede you noght to been a cokewold;
For filthe and eelde, also moot I thee,   1215
Been grete wardeyns upon chastitee.
But nathelees, syn I knowe youre delit,
I shal fulfille youre worldly appetit.

1203 **spectacle:** eyeglass
1209 **gentils:** nobles
1212 **auctours:** authoritative writers   **fynden:** find (to support this)
1214 **cokewold:** cuckold
1215 **thee:** prosper
1216 **wardeyns:** guardians
1217 **delit:** desire

"Chese now," quod she, "oon of thise thynges
      tweye:
To han me foul and old til that I deye,   1220
And be to yow a trewe, humble wyf,
And nevere yow displese in al my lyf,
Or elles ye wol han me yong and fair,
And take youre aventure of the repair
That shal be to youre hous by cause of me,
Or in som oother place, may wel be.   1226
Now chese yourselven, wheither that yow
      liketh."
    This knyght avyseth hym and sore siketh,
But atte laste he seyde in this manere:
"My lady and my love, and wyf so deere,   1230
I put me in youre wise governance;
Cheseth youreself which may be moost ples-
      ance
And moost honour to yow and me also.
I do no fors the wheither of the two,
For as yow liketh, it suffiseth me."   1235
    "Thanne have I gete of yow maistrie," quod
      she,

1224 **aventure:** chances **repair:** resort, visitors
1227 **wheither:** which
1234 **I do no fors:** I don't care
1235 **suffiseth me:** is sufficient for me

"Syn I may chese and governe as me lest?"

"Ye, certes, wyf," quod he, "I holde it best."

"Kys me," quod she, "we be no lenger wrothe,
For, by my trouthe, I wol be to yow bothe—
This is to seyn, ye, bothe fair and good.   1241
I prey to God that I moote sterven wood,
But I to yow be also good and trewe
As evere was wyf, syn that the world was newe.
And but I be to-morn as fair to seene   1245
As any lady, emperice, or queene,
That is bitwixe the est and eke the west,
Dooth with my lyf and deth right as yow lest.
Cast up the curtyn, looke how that it is."

And whan the knyght saugh verraily al this,
That she so fair was, and so yong therto,   1251
For joye he heme hire in his armes two.
His herte bathed in a bath of blisse.
A thousand tyme a-rewe he gan hire kisse,
And she obeyed hym in every thyng   1255
That myghte doon hym plesance or likyng.

And thus they lyve unto hir lyves ende
In parfit joye; and Jhesu Crist us sende

1242 **sterven wood:** die insane
1245 **to-morn:** in the morning
1253 **bathed:** basked
1254 **a-rewe:** in succession

Housbondes meeke, yonge, and fressh abedde,
And grace t'overbyde hem that we wedde;
And eek I praye Jhesu shorte hir lyves   1261
That noght wol be governed by hir wyves;
And olde and angry nygardes of dispence,
God sende hem soone verray pestilence!

Heere endeth the Wyves Tale of Bathe.

1260 **t'overbyde:** to outlive

Chaucer's Retraction

Now preye I to hem alle that herkne this litel tretys
or rede, that if ther be any thyng in it that liketh
hem, that therof they thanken oure Lord Jhesu
Crist, of whom procedeth al wit and al good-
nesse./ And if ther be any thyng that displese
hem, I preye hem also that they arrette it to the
defaute of myn unkonnynge and nat to my wyl,
that wolde ful fayn have seyd bettre if I hadde
had konnynge./ For oure book seith, "Al that is
writen is written for oure doctrine," and that is
myn entente./ Wherfore I biseke yow mekely, for
the mercy of God, that ye preye for me that Crist
have mercy on me and foryeve me my giltes;/
and namely of my translacions and enditynges
of worldly vanitees, the whiche I revoke in my

1265 **this litel tretys:** the preceding tale.
1266 **arrette:** attribute

retracciouns:/ as is the book of Troilus; the book   1270
also of Fame; the book of the XXV. Ladies; the
book of the Duchesse; the book of Seint Valen-
tynes day of the Parlement of Briddes; the tales
of Caunterbury, thilke that sownen into synne;/
the book of the Leoun; and many another book,
if they were in my remembrance, and many a
song and many a leccherous lay, that Crist for his
grete mercy foryeve me the synne./ But of the
translacion of Boece de Consolacione, and oth-
ere bookes of legendes of seintes, and omelies,
and moralitee, and devocioun,/ that thanke I oure
Lord Jhesu Crist and his blisful Mooder, and alle
the seintes of hevene,/ bisekynge hem that they
from hennes forth unto my lyves ende sende me
grace to biwayle my giltes and to studie to the
salvacioun of my soule, and graunte me grace of
verray penitence, confessioun and satisfaccioun to
doon in this present lyf,/ thurgh the benigne grace
of hym that is kyng of kynges and preest over alle
preestes, that boghte us with the precious blood of
his herte,/ so that I may been oon of hem at the

1270 **book of the XXV. Ladies:** The Legend of Good Women
1270 **sownen into synne:** tend toward, are conducive to, sin.
1271 **book of the Leoun:** a lost work.

day of doom that shulle be saved. *Qui cum Patre et*   1276
Spiritu Sancto vivit et regnat Deus per omnia secula.
Amen.

Heere is ended the book of the tales of Caunterbury,
compiled by Geffrey Chaucer, of whos soule Jhesu
Crist have mercy. Amen.

1276 ***Qui cum Patre . . . Amen***: He who lives and reigns with the Father and the Holy Spirit, God, world without end. Amen.

Acknowledgments

Thank you to Yvonne Bailey-Smith, Ben Bailey-Smith, Luke Smith, Nick Laird and Indhu Rubasingham for the early reads and edits.

Thank you to Carolyn Cooper CD, Professor of Literary and Cultural Studies at the University of the West Indies, Mona, Jamaica, for her edits, insight and time.